Cambridge Elements ≡

Elements in the Philosophy of Science
edited by
Robert Northcott
Birkbeck, University of London
Jacob Stegenga
University of Cambridge

PHILOSOPHY OF PROBABILITY AND STATISTICAL MODELLING

Mauricio Suárez
Complutense University of Madrid

CAMBRIDGE
UNIVERSITY PRESS

CAMBRIDGE
UNIVERSITY PRESS

University Printing House, Cambridge CB2 8BS, United Kingdom

One Liberty Plaza, 20th Floor, New York, NY 10006, USA

477 Williamstown Road, Port Melbourne, VIC 3207, Australia

314–321, 3rd Floor, Plot 3, Splendor Forum, Jasola District Centre, New Delhi – 110025, India

79 Anson Road, #06–04/06, Singapore 079906

Cambridge University Press is part of the University of Cambridge.

It furthers the University's mission by disseminating knowledge in the pursuit of education, learning, and research at the highest international levels of excellence.

www.cambridge.org
Information on this title: www.cambridge.org/9781108984942
DOI: 10.1017/9781108985826

First published 2020

A catalogue record for this publication is available from the British Library.

ISBN 978-1-108-98494-2 Paperback
ISSN 2517-7273 (online)
ISSN 2517-7265 (print)

Philosophy of Probability and Statistical Modelling

Elements in the Philosophy of Science

DOI: 10.1017/9781108985826
First published online: December 2020

Mauricio Suárez
Complutense University of Madrid
Author for correspondence: Mauricio Suárez, msuarez@filos.ucm.es

Abstract: This Element has two main aims. The first one (Sections 1–7) is a historically informed review of the philosophy of probability. It describes recent historiography, lays out the distinction between subjective and objective notions, and concludes by applying the historical lessons to the main interpretations of probability. The second aim (Sections 8–13) focuses entirely on objective probability and advances a number of novel theses regarding its role in scientific practice. A distinction is drawn between traditional attempts to interpret chance, and a novel methodological study of its application. A radical form of pluralism is then introduced, advocating a tripartite distinction between propensities, probabilities, and frequencies. Finally, a distinction is drawn between two different applications of chance in statistical modelling which, it is argued, vindicates the overall methodological approach. The ensuing conception of objective probability in practice is the 'complex nexus of chance'.

Keywords: Philosophy of Science, Philosophy of Probability, Philosophy of Statistical Modeling

ISBNs: 9781108984942 (PB), 9781108985826 (OC)
ISSNs: 2517-7273 (online), 2517-7265 (print)

Contents

Introduction

Humans have been thinking in probabilistic terms since antiquity. They have been thinking systematically and philosophizing about probability since the seventeenth century. And they have been formalizing probability since the end of the nineteenth century. The twentieth century saw intense philosophical work done on *interpreting* probability, in a sort of attempt to find out its essence. The twenty-first century, I argue, will bring a focus on more practical endeavours, concerning mainly the methodologies of data analysis and statistical modelling. The essence of probability, it turns out, lies in the diversity of its uses. So, the methodological study of the use of probability is what brings humans closer to a comprehensive understanding of its nature.

These and other ideas expounded in this Element developed out of a Marie Curie project on probability and propensities that I carried out at the Institute of Philosophy of the School of Advanced Study at London University during 2013–15. I came out of that project with the distinct impression that the study of practice was of primary importance; and that much philosophy of probability is still to come to terms with it. This Element is my first attempt at the bare bones of a new research programme into the methodology of statistical modelling. Most of the Element is devoted to justifying this methodology – on the grounds of practical involvement with the scientific modelling practice but also, I argue, on account of the limitations of the traditional interpretative approaches to the topic.

Thus, the first half of the Element (Sections 1–7) is entirely a state-of-the-art review of the historiography of probability and its ensuing impact upon the interpretative endeavour. This is fitting for a Cambridge *Elements* volume, which allows for a profuse setting of the stage. And it is anyway needed in order to understand why nothing other than a study of the practice of statistical model building will do for a full understanding of objective probability. I first explore (in Section 1) the dual character of the notion of probability from its inception – the subjective and objective aspects of probability that are essential to any understanding the concept. The twentieth century brought in several *interpretations* of probability. But one way or another, they all aim to reduce probability to either subjective or objective elements, thus doing away with the duality; and one way or another they all fail, precisely because they do away with the duality. In the remaining sections in this half of the Element, I analyse in detail the many objections against both the main subjective interpretations (the logical and personalist or Bayesian interpretations), and the main objective interpretations (the frequency and propensity interpretations). To make most of these interpretations work, and overcome the objections, demands some acknowledgment of the complex duality of probability. This is by now widely accepted, and the Element first reviews the roots and consequences of pluralism about objective probability.

The second half of the Element (Sections 8–13) then centres upon the objective aspects of probability, but now without any pretence of a reduction of the whole concept. The discussion is focused entirely on objective probability, and it contains most of the original material. I advance a number of novel theses, which I defend in various original ways as well as proposing a number of new avenues for research. The starting point is pluralist, and it accepts the duality insofar as it argues that there are important matters of judgement in the selection of crucial aspects of the application of objective probability in practice. Here, the critical distinction, advanced in Sections 8 and 9, is between the traditional project to merely *interpret* probability and a distinct project to study the *application* of probability. On the other hand, I go considerably beyond the pluralism defended in the first half of the Element and, in Section 10, I embrace novel forms of pluralism and pragmatism regarding objective probability.

The central idea of the second half, which also informs the Element as a whole and looms large through most of its discussions, is what I have elsewhere called the 'tripartite conception' of objective probability (Suárez, 2017a). This is the idea that the failure to reduce chance to either propensity or frequency ought to lead to the acceptance of all three concepts as distinct, insufficient yet necessary, parts of the larger notion of 'objective probability'. This tripartite conception is introduced in Section 10, which also assesses the role of judgement and various subjective components. Sections 11, 12, and 13 are then devoted to modelling methodology, and the application of the tripartite conception in statistical modelling practice in particular, in what I call the 'complex nexus of chance' (CNC). The thought running through these sections is new and radical: objective probability is constituted by a thick array of interlinked practices in its application; these are practices that essentially involve the three distinct notions pointed to above; and since none of these notions is theoretically reducible to any combination or set of the other two, this means that the overall methodology remains unavoidably 'complex'. There is no philosophical theory that may explicate fully the concept of objective probability, or chance, by reducing this complexity, and this already sheds light on the limitations of the interpretations reviewed in the Element's first half.

What's more, the second half of the Element also continues to illustrate the fundamental duality of probability unearthed in the historiographical material reviewed in the first seven sections. It does so in three different yet interrelated ways. First of all, it leaves open that subjective elements may come into the nature of the single-case chances that make up the tripartite conception.

Secondly, confirmation theory comes into the assessment of evidence for and against different models. And, finally, there are irreducible subjective judgements involved in the pragmatist methodology advocated in the later sections. For instance, in Section 11 I argue that choosing the appropriate parametrization of the phenomenon to be modelled is a critical part; and there is no algorithm or automatic procedure to do this – the choice of free parameters is subject to some fundamentally 'subjective' estimate of what is most appropriate in the context for the purposes of the model at hand. Once again, the 'subjective' and the 'objective' aspects of probability meet in fundamental ways (see Gelman and Hennig (2017) as well as my response Suárez (2017b) for an account of such a merge in practice). Another related sense of subjectivism in statistical modelling is sometimes referred to as the 'art of statistical modelling' and concerns the choice of a correlative outcome or attribute space. There is nothing arbitrary about this 'subjectivity' though, since it answers precisely to specific pragmatic constraints: it is a highly contextual and purpose-driven judgement.

On my view, each of the parametrizations of a phenomenon involves a description of its propensities, dispositions, or causal powers. What is relevant about propensities is that they do not fall in the domain of the chance functions that they generate (Suárez, 2018). Rather a propensity is related to a chance function in the way that possibilities are related to probabilities: the propensity sets the range of possible outcomes, the full description of the outcome space, while the chance function defined over this space then determines the precise single-case chance ascribed to each of these outcomes. A different parametrization would involve a different description of the system's propensities, perhaps at a different level of generality or abstraction (and no parametrization is infinitely precise); and focusing on a different set of propensities may well issue in a different set of possible outcomes, hence a different outcome space, over which a different chance function shall lay out its probabilities. Since the parametrizations obey pragmatic constraints that require appropriate judgements within the context of application, it follows that the outcome spaces will correspondingly depend on such judgements. In other words, a chance function is not just a description of objective probabilities for objectively possible outcomes; it is one amongst many such descriptions for a particular system, made relevant by appropriate judgements of salience, always within a particular context of inquiry. Here, again, the 'subjective' and the 'objective' aspects of probability merge.

1 The Archaeology of Probability

The philosophy of probability is a well-established field within the philosophy of science, which focuses upon questions regarding the nature and interpretation of the notion of probability, the connections between probability and metaphysical chance, and the role that the notion of probability plays in statistical modelling practice across the sciences. Philosophical reflection upon probability is as old as the concept of probability itself, which historians tend to place originally in the late seventeenth century. As the concept developed, it also acquired increasing formal precision, culminating in the so-called Kolmogorov axioms first formulated in 1933. Ever since, philosophical discussions regarding the interpretation of probability have often been restricted to the interpretation of this formal mathematical concept, yet the history of the concept of probability is enormously rich and varied. I thus begin with a review of some of the relevant history, heavily indebted to Ian Hacking's (Hacking, 1975, 1990) and Lorraine Daston's (Daston, 1988) accounts. Throughout this historical review I emphasize the non-eliminability of objective chance. I then turn to a detailed description of the different views on the nature of probability, beginning with the classical interpretation (often ascribed to Laplace, and anticipated by Leibniz), and then moving on to the logical interpretation (Keynes), the subjective interpretation (Ramsey, De Finetti), the frequency interpretation (Mises, Reichenbach), and ending in a detailed analysis of the propensity interpretation in many of its variants (including the views of Peirce, Popper, Mellor, Gillies, and my own contributions). The discussion is driven by the 'doctrine of chances' and the recognition that objective chance is an ineliminable and essential dimension of our contemporary concept of probability. In particular I argue that the logical and subjective interpretations require for their intelligibility a notion of objective chance and that the frequency interpretation is motivated by a form of empiricism that is in tension with an honest and literal realism about objective chance.

Hacking's archaeology of probability revealed unsuspected layers of meaning in the term 'probability', unearthed a fundamental duality in the concept, and revealed that, although the concept itself in its modern guise only fully appears around 1660 (most notably in the Pascal–Fermat correspondence), the imprint of the antecedent marks (i.e. of the 'prehistory' of probability) are even to this day considerable. The legacy of Hacking's inquiries into probability is an increased understanding of the transformative processes that turned the Renaissance's concept of 'probability' into our contemporary concept of probability. The new concept finally comes through strongly in the writings of the Jansenist members of Port Royal (mainly Arnauld and Pascal), but it has both antecedents and contemporaries in some of leading thinkers on signs, chance, and evidence, including Paracelsus, Fracastoro, Galileo, Gassendi, and most notably the contemporaneous Leibniz and Huygens.

The fundamental change traced by Hacking concerns the notion of evidence which, in its contemporary sense, also emerges at around the same time. In the old order, the justification of 'probable' claims was thought to be provided by the testimony of authority (usually religious authority). But the Renaissance brings along a reading of natural and, in particular, medical and physiological phenomena where certain 'signs' are taken to impart a corresponding testimony, under the authority of the book of nature. 'Probable' is then whatever is warranted by the relevant authority in the interpretation of the 'signs' of nature. But what to do in cases of conflict of authorities? Hacking (1975, ch. 5) chronicles the fascinating dispute between the Jesuit casuistry tradition – which considers the consequences of each authority and chooses accordingly – and the protesting Jansenists' novel emphasis on locating the one true testimony – typically the testimony provided by nature herself. The transformation of the testimony of earthily authority into the evidence of nature thus configures the background to the emergence of probability. Hacking's careful 'archaeology' then reveals that the most striking imprint of the old order upon the new is the dualistic or Janus-faced character of probability. Our modern concept of probability is born around 1660 and characteristically exhibits both epistemological and ontological aspects. It inherits the dualism from the medieval and Renaissance conceptual schemes which, however otherwise fundamentally different, also exhibited a similar dual-ity. Thus, in the old order and parlance, 'probable' stood roughly for both the opinion of the authority and the evidence of nature's signs, while in the parlance of the new order, 'probable' stands both for logical or subjective degree of belief and for objective chance, tendency or disposition.

My aim in the first half of the Element is to review the present state of the philosophy of probability with an eye on this fundamental duality or pluralism. I shall emphasize how an appropriate articulation of subjective probability is facilitated by a proper regard for the objective dimension of probability. And conversely, a fair theory of objective chance needs to make room and accommodate subjective elements. First, in Section 2 I continue the historical review by introducing the notion of equipossibility in Leibniz and Laplace. I then move on in Section 3 to the logical interpretation and the principle of indifference as they appear mainly in the work of John Maynard Keynes. In both cases I aim to show the role of objective notions of probability in the background of the argument and development of the logical interpretation of probability. In Section 4 I follow a similar strategy with the subjective interpretation of Ramsey and De Finetti, in an attempt to display the ways in which the interpret-ation ultimately calls for objective notions in order to overcome its difficulties. Section 5 retakes the historical account in order to review the history of metaphysical chance and its ultimate vindication in the late nineteenth century, particularly in relation to the work of the American pragmatist philosopher, Charles Peirce. In Section 6 I introduce and review different versions of the frequency interpretation of probability (finite frequentism and hypothetical frequentism). I show that subjective notions appear in the formulation of these theories, or at any rate in those formulations that manage to overcome the objections. Finally, in Section 7, I review in detail some of the main propensity accounts of probability, pointing out some of their resorts to subjective notions.

2 The Classical Interpretation: Equipossibility

The classical interpretation of probability is supposed to be first enunciated in the works of Pierre Simon Laplace, in particular in his influential *Essai Philosophique sur les Probabilités* (1814). But there are important antecedents to both classical probability and the notion of equipossibility that ground it in the writings of many of the seventeenth-century probabilists,[1] particularly Leibniz's and Bernouilli's about a century earlier. Ian Hacking (1975) chronicles the appearance of the notion of equipossibility in the metaphysical writings of Leibniz, and the connection is apposite since it is an essentially modal notion that nowadays can best be understood by means of possible world semantics. I first review the historical developments that give rise to the Laplacean definition, and only then address some of the difficulties with the classical view in more contemporary terms.

Leibniz seems to have developed his views on probability against the background of an antecedent distinction between two types of possibility, which roughly coincide with our present-day notions of *de re* and *de dicto* possibility (Hacking, 1975, p. 124). In English we mark the distinction between epistemological and physical possibilities by means of different prepositions on the word 'possible'. There is first a 'possible that' epistemological modality: 'It is possible that Laplace just adopted Leibniz's distinction' expresses an epistemological possibility; for all we know it remains possible that Laplace did in fact copy Leibniz's distinction. The statement is in the present because it reflects our own lack of knowledge now. Contrast it with the following 'possible for' statement: 'It was possible for Laplace to adopt Leibniz's distinction' expresses a physical possibility at Laplace's time, namely that Laplace had the resources at his disposal, and sufficient access to Leibniz's work, and was not in any other way physically impeded from reproducing the distinction in his own work. More prosaic examples abound: 'It is possible that my child rode his bicycle' is

---

[1] Gigerenzer et al. (1989, ch. 1.9) even argue that by the time of Poisson's subsequent writings circa 1837, the classical interpretation was already in decline!

epistemological, while 'it is possible for my child to ride his bicycle' is physical, and so on.

Now, epistemological possibility is typically *de dicto* (it pertains to what we know or state), while ontological possibility is *de re* (it pertains to how things are in the world independently of what we say or state about it). So, the 'possible that' phrase tends to express a *de dicto* possibility, while the 'possible for' phrase expresses *de re* possibilities. The two are obviously related – for one physical possibility may be thought to be a precondition for epistemological possibility since there is no *de dicto* without *de re*. For Leibniz the connection was, if anything, stricter – they were two sides of the same concept of possibility. And in building his notion of probability out of possibility, Leibniz transferred this dualism onto the very concept of probability: 'Quod facile est in re, id probabile est in mente' (quoted in Hacking, 1975, p. 128). The link expresses Leibniz's belief that the dual physical and epistemological aspects of probability track the duality of *de re* and *de dicto* possibility.

This tight conceptual connection is also the source of Leibniz's emphasis on equipossibility as the grounds for the allocation of equal probabilities, and it in turn underwrites Bernouilli's and Laplace's similar uses of the notion. Leibniz employs two separate arguments for the equiprobability of equipossible events: the first derives from the principle of sufficient reason and is essentially epistemological; the other one derives from physical causality and is essentially ontological or physical (Hacking, 1975, p. 127). According to the first, if we cannot find any reason for one outcome to be any more 'possible' than another, we judge them epistemically equiprobable. According to the latter, if none of the outcomes is in fact more 'facile' than any other, they are physically equiprobable.

The duality of probability (and its grounding in the similar duality of possibility) becomes gradually lost in the advent of the classical interpretation of probability, which is often presented in a purely epistemic fashion, as asserting that probabilities represent merely our lack of knowledge. The eighteenth century brought an increasing emphasis on the underlying determinism of random looking phenomena, in the wake of Newtonian dynamics, and probability in such a deterministic universe can only signal the imperfection of our knowledge. By the time of the publication of the treatise that established the classical interpretation (i.e. Laplace's *Essai sur les Probabilités*) in 1814, the deterministic paradigm had become so imperious, and the demise of probability to the strict confines of the epistemology so marked, that Laplace could confidently assert that a superior omniscient intelligence would have no time or purpose for probability. If so, the fact that ordinary agents have use for nontrivial (i.e. other than 0 or 1) probabilities comes to show our cognitive limitations and entails that probability is essentially an epistemic consequence of our ignorance. The connection is at the foundation of subjective views on probability and is nowadays embodied in what is known as *Laplace's demon*: 'an intelligence which at a certain moment would know all forces that set nature in motion, and all positions of all items of which nature is composed, if this intelligence were also vast enough to submit these data to analysis, she would embrace in a single formula the movements of the greatest bodies of the universe and those of the tiniest atom; for such an intelligence nothing would be uncertain and the future just like the past would be present before her eyes' (Laplace, 1814, p. 4, my own translation).

Yet, the Laplacean formal definition of probability as the ratio of favourable to possible cases, of course, only makes sense against the background of equipossible events, as: $P(a) = \frac{\#(a)}{\#(t)}$ where #(a) is the number of positive cases of a, and #(t) is the number of total cases. Thus, in the case of an unbiased coin, the probability of the coin landing heads if tossed is given by the ratio of the cases in which it lands heads divided by the total number of cases (i.e. either outcome). But this, of course, assumes that each case is equipossible – that is, that the tosses are independent in the strong sense of there being no causal influences that determine different degrees of possibility for the different outcomes. If, for instance, landing heads on the first trial made it more likely for the coin to land heads in the second trial, the probability of heads in the second or any other trial in the series would not be given by the ratio. Laplace himself was acutely aware of the issue. As he writes: 'The preceding notion of probability supposes that, in increasing in the same ratio the number of favourable cases and that of all the cases possible, the probability remains the same' (Laplace, 1814, ch. 6).

Commentators through the years have pointed out repeatedly how any purely epistemic reading of the condition of equipossibility would render Laplace's definition of probability hopelessly circular: it defines the notion of probability back in terms of the equivalent notion of equal possibility – the very grounds for epistemic equiprobability. Hence, we find Hans Reichenbach (1935/1949, p. 353) stating as part of his critique of epistemological theories: 'Cases that satisfy the principle of "no reason to the contrary" are said to be equipossible and therefore equiprobable. This addition certainly does not improve the argument, even if it originates with a mathematician as eminent as Laplace, since it obviously represents a vicious circle. Equipossible is equivalent to equiprobable.' However, the realization that Leibniz and Bernouilli in fact entertained mixed notions of probability and possibility, incorporating both epistemic and ontological dimensions, allows for a distinct resolution of this issue. If the equipossibility is ontological, if, for example, it is physically there in nature, then the assumption of equal probabilities follows without any appeal to sufficient reason. There seems to be no circularity involved here as long as physical possibility may be independently understood.

Our standard contemporary understanding of modality is in terms of possible world semantics. A statement of possibility is understood as a statement about what is the case in some possible world, which may but need not be the actual world. Equipossibility is trickier since it involves comparisons across possible worlds, and these are notoriously hard to pin down quantitatively. Measures of similarity are sometimes used. For two statements of possibility to be quantitatively equivalent it needs to be the case, for example, that the number of possible worlds that make them true be the same, or that the 'distance' of such worlds from the actual world be the same, or that the similarity of those worlds to the actual world be quantitatively identical. Whichever measure is adopted, it does seem to follow that some objective relation across worlds warrants a claim as to identical probability. The quantitative measures of equipossibility are not necessarily probability measures – but they can be seen 'to inject' a probability measure at least with respect to the equally possible alternatives. It is at least intuitive that physical equipossibility may give rise to equiprobability without circularity. The upshot is that what looks like an eminently reasonable purely epistemological definition of probability as the ratio of favourable to possible cases in fact presupposes a fair amount of ontology – and a concomitantly robust and unusually finely graded notion of objective physical possibility.

3 The Logical Interpretation: Indifference

There are two schools of thought that assume that probability is not objective or ontological – not a matter of what the facts of the world are, but rather a matter of the mind – one of our understanding or knowledge of the world. These accounts follow the main lines of the most common interpretation of the classical theory. According to the logical interpretation, probability is a matter of the logical relations between propositions – a question thus regarding the relational properties of propositions. According to the subjective interpretation, by contrast, probability is a matter of our degrees of belief – a question that regards therefore our mental states, and in particular our belief states. These interpretations developed particularly during the twentieth century. The logical interpretation was championed by John Maynard Keynes, Harold Jeffreys, and Rudolf Carnap (for what Carnap called probability$_1$ statements, which he distinguished from objective probability$_2$ statements); while the subjective interpretation was defended by Frank Ramsey, Bruno de Finetti, and Leonard

Savage. In this section I review the logical interpretation, mainly as espoused by Keynes, and in Section 4 I look at the subjective interpretation, particularly in Ramsey's version.

Keynes argues that probability is a logical relation between propositions akin to logical entailment but weaker – whereby two propositions A and B are related by means of logical entailment if and only if A cannot be true and B fail to be so; while A and B are more weakly related by partial degree of entailment if and only if A cannot be true and B fail to have some probability, however short of certainty, or probability one. So, the first caveat that must be introduced at this point is the fact that for Keynes probability is not in fact subjective but objective. However, we must be careful with our use of language here – 'objective' for Keynes does not stand for 'ontological' but for non-arbitrary or relative to known fact. More particularly, Keynes held that the probability of a proposition is always the relation of partial degree of entailment of that proposition by some background body of knowledge. That is, given some background knowledge, a proposition is entailed to a certain degree. As he writes (Keynes, 1921, p. 4): 'In the sense important to logic, probability is not subjective. It is not, that is to say, subject to human caprice. A proposition is not probable because we think it so. Once the facts are given that determine our knowledge, what is probable or improbable in these circumstances has been fixed objectively, and it is independent of our opinion.'

The fundamental insight here is the thought that probability is a logical relation amongst propositions. Thus, if I claim now that 'the probability that it will rain tomorrow is 50 per cent', I am making a claim about how probable this proposition is on account of the knowledge I now have of any facts relative to it – weather patterns, dynamical laws, the present isobaric facts, and so on. If and when my information changes, so does my probability estimate. But this is perfectly consistent with the relational character of probability: it is always a property of a proposition relative to background knowledge, which will naturally vary with time, as new information accrues. Therefore, the probability of the proposition in question becomes zero or one not at the time the event comes to be – or fails to be – but rather at the time we as agents gain the relevant background information. Yet, there is a normative dimension to probability according to Keynes, as we saw in the quote above. What this means is that there is some background information that is objectively relevant at each time for each proposition. The rational agent is normatively constrained by it in the sense that, were the agent to be aware of all the relevant facts, she would ascribe the corresponding probability. We can thus say that objectively the probability of the proposition is given by its relation to the background facts that are relevant to our knowledge *regardless of whether anyone is in fact aware or not of those facts*. The knower's contribution is in the relevance of the facts, not so much in the objective relation those facts hold to the proposition in question. This observation is not without consequence for any logical concept of probability – or in fact any inductive logic more generally (i.e. any logic that attempts to capture the non-deductive or demonstrative patterns of inference characteristic of inductive learning).

The main rule of probabilistic inference in a logical conception of probability is the so-called *principle of indifference*, a contemporary refinement of Leibniz's principle of sufficient reason. It was clear since Leibniz that probabilities can only be quantified numerically to the extent that some of the alternatives may be regarded as equiprobable. Where Leibniz has spoken of 'having no sufficient reason' to assert one alternative as more probable than another, Keynes instead says (1921, p. 41) that 'the principle of indifference asserts that if there is no known reason for predicating of our subject one rather than another of several alternatives, then relatively to such knowledge the assertions of each of these alternatives have an *equal* probability'. Thus, the application of Leibniz's principle may seem circular, but Keynes' statement is coherently non-circular. Critically and specifically, the conditions for equiprobability here do not appeal to probability itself. 'Predicating of our subject one rather than another of several alternatives' does not imply taking one to be more probable than another. It just implies predication in a particular context, or relative to certain background knowledge.

Thus, suppose we have no reason to believe a particular coin is biased – it seems then reasonable to give both possible outcomes of a tossing trial equal probability = ½. The subject here is the outcome of the tossing of this particular coin; the alternatives are the two different ways in which it may land; relative to our present knowledge, there is no reason to 'predicate' of the subject that it may be heads any more than there is reason to predicate that it may be tails. It is then legitimate to apply the principle of indifference and ascribe equal probabilities to both outcomes. Similar kinds of reasoning apply to all kinds of games of chance, including dice or roulette.

Nonetheless, there are well-known problems with the application of the principle.[2] Most of these problems appear in the context of further divisions of the possible alternatives that result in numerically impossible or contradictory applications of the principle. A well-known example involves a coloured object, say a book, whose colour we ignore, surrounded by other objects coloured red; we may come to the conclusion, on applying the principle of

---

[2] See, in particular, Keynes (1921, ch. 4 §§ 4–9); the main problems are nicely recapitulated in Gillies (2000, ch. 4). Some of these problems go back to objections famously first raised by Bertrand (1889) and Borel (1909).

indifference in complete ignorance as to its colour, that the probability that it is red is ½, while the probability that it is not red is also ½. In this case, the alternatives we may predicate of our subject are 'red' / 'non-red'. However, it should be obvious that there are many subdivisions of 'non-red' into all the different colours of the spectrum, and the probability ascriptions can therefore be very different depending on what subdivisions are considered. For instance, the set of 'non-red' objects may be taken to include all 'yellow' objects, and those 'non-yellow' objects that are also 'non-red'. We then get ascriptions of probability ½ to 'red' and 'non-red', and probability ¼ to both 'yellow' and 'non-red and non-yellow' which seems bizarre to say the least, since we could have similarly subdivided along any other different partition. Worse still, we could have initially entertained a different array of colours such as black versus non-black, or blue versus non-blue, thus rendering probability (red) = probability (black) = probability (blue) = ½, yet obviously probability (red) + probability (blue) + probability (black) $\neq$ ½ + ½ + ½ = $^3/_2$, since probability (any colour) = 1. So, the application of the principle of indifference to different partitions simultaneously yields a logical contradiction. (Keynes helpfully points out (Keynes 1921, § 4) that the assumption that no object can be simultaneously two different colours is not itself part of the principle of indifference, since it concerns not the subject – the book, but the predicate – the colours.)

More examples can be easily generated, and multiply; Bertrand famously showed how to generate geometrical paradoxes with classical probability under the assumption of the principle of indifference – and these are nowadays known as 'Bertrand's paradoxes'. Bertrand's original paradox (Bertrand, 1889; see also Gillies, 2000, ch. 4) concerns the inscription of an equilateral triangle in a circle. The exercise is then to choose any chord of the circle at random (i.e. any line from one point on the circumference to another) and calculate the probability that it is longer than a side of the triangle. There are, however, many ways to compute this probability. Bertrand canvasses three: (i) rotate the triangle until one of its vertices coincides with one of the end points of the chord, then check for the length of the chord against the side of the triangle; assuming indifference, compute the probability for any arbitrary chord as a linear measure of the length of the arc smaller or longer than the side of the triangle; the resulting probability that the chord is longer is ⅓. (ii) Check against the radius of the circumference that lies perpendicularly to the side of the triangle; assuming indifference, compute the probability as a linear measure of the length of the radius before and after it meets the side of the triangle; the resulting probability is ½. Finally, (iii) draw a concentric inner circle within the larger circle at radius ½ of the total radius of the circle; its area is therefore ¼ of the total area of the circle; then pick a point on the larger circle and draw a chord at random, assuming indifference; the probability that the chord is longer than the side of the triangle is the probability that it lies in the inner circle, which is ¼.

In other words, indifference generates different values for the probabilities of particular events, depending on the partitions or classes of events that are considered. There is a similar problem for frequency accounts, namely the reference class problem, as we shall see. Notice, however, that here probability is not defined with respect to the class, unlike in the case of frequencies, but entirely with respect to an underlying measure of indifference. It just so happens that the measure critically depends on the partitions. Notice also that in Bertrand's geometrical paradoxes, the generating function of the partitions is continuous – the length of the arc; the first and simplest case by contrast works on the assumption that there is only a finite and discrete number of colours. While the paradox seems identical in both cases, its resolution in fact greatly differs for each case.

Keynes realized that the simplest form of the paradox for discrete finite events has a resolution within the confines of the principle of indifference. It requires us to accept a principle that would select the narrowest possible class available to us – which Carnap (1950, pp. 138ff) went on to describe as analogous to his own *principle of total evidence*: 'A principle which seems generally recognized, although not always obeyed, says that if we wish to apply such a theorem of the theory of probability to a given knowledge situation, then we have to take as evidence the total evidence available to the person in question at the time in question, that is to say, his total knowledge of the results of his observations.' As regards the finite discrete case, this entails that we use the narrowest class that we have available; 'non-red' is not suitable when we have 'blue', 'yellow', and so on, available and so can classify the object accordingly.

Keynes (1921, p. 55) refers to such judgements as judgements of 'relevance' and enunciates the modified version of the principle as follows: 'There must be no relevant evidence relating to one alternative, unless there is corresponding evidence relating to the other; our relevant evidence, that is to say, must be symmetrical with regard to the alternatives, and must be applicable to each in the same manner.' Then, in a series of crucial subsequent qualifications of this statement he first adds (Keynes, 1921, p. 60) that: 'there should be a formal rule that will exclude those cases in which one of the alternatives involved is itself a disjunction of sub-alternatives of the same form', and then he gives an appropriate formalization of this rule in terms of propositional functions ϕ (a_r). Finally, he critically adds the proviso that a necessary condition on the application of the principle of indifference is that these alternatives and sub-alternatives considered 'should be, relatively to the evidence, indivisible'. In other words, the principle of indifference is also legitimately to be applied to indivisible finite sub-alternatives of any subject for which there is no distinguishing relevant evidence. It should be obvious that evidence for 'red' is not also relevant evidence for 'non-red', or vice versa. That is, the kind of observational evidence that may relevantly distinguish 'red' is also relevant for 'blue' or 'yellow' but not for the larger divisible alternatives such as 'non-red' and so on.

Keynes' modified principle of indifference is thus applicable to the 'book paradox' and can in principle overcome at least many of the paradoxes relative to the finite discrete case. It is widely believed, however, that it cannot overcome Bertrand-style geometrical paradoxes in the real number continuum (Gillies, 2000, Ch. 3.5; Rowbottom, 2013). The reason is simply that the qualification introduced by Keynes makes the principle essentially inapplicable to the continuum cases, for which the application of 'indivisible' does not hold for any given interval. And no singular development or additional qualification seems to render it applicable. Since a very large number of statistical probabilities require the real number continuum,[3] this does entail that the notion of logical probability, and the principle of indifference at its core, has very limited applicability.

4 The Subjective Interpretation: Credence

Frank Ramsey was one of Keynes' disciples at Cambridge and famously subjected Keynes' logical interpretation to a searching critique. He complained that he could not in any way ascertain or detect the logical relationship that purportedly makes up probability. While logical consequence or demonstrative reasoning is self-evident, this is not the case for probabilistic reasoning or inference, which is not evident in the same way. As Ramsey famously put it (Ramsey, 1926, p. 161): '[T]here really do not seem to be any such things as the probability relations that he [Keynes] describes. He supposes that, at any rate in certain cases, they can be perceived; but speaking for myself I feel confident that this is not true. I do not perceive them, and if I am to be persuaded that they exist it must be by argument; moreover I shrewdly suspect that others do not perceive them either, because they are able to come to so very little agreement as to which of them relates any two given propositions'. Ramsey instead proposed to understand probability as personal degree of belief. That is, according to Ramsey, the probability of a proposition is a measure of the strength of a rational partial degree in the proposition. More particularly, Ramsey set out to show that probabilities can always be interpreted subjectively, on the one

---

[3] And indeed the contemporary notion of mathematical probability, which defines probability as a mapping from a set of propositions to the real unit interval, thus allowing for an infinite set of properties and subdivisions.

hand, and on the other hand that subjective degrees of belief, if they are rational, must conform to the axioms of probability. In other words he set out to show an identity claim between probabilities and partial degrees of belief.

Ramsey's identity claim is the first in a series that I review in later sections of this Element, including Reichenbach's identity conception, which identifies probabilities with frequencies, and Popper's 'identity thesis' – as referred to in Suárez (2013) – which identifies probabilities and propensities. These identity claims all have a fundamental intent to *reduce* probability, which they consider suspect on a number of grounds, to notions that are supposed to be more legitimate or acceptable, often on empiricist grounds. Thus, Ramsey thought that agents' degrees of belief are essentially measurable directly by experiments – and thus accessible in a way that probabilities as theoretical formal entities are not. Similarly, as we shall see in later sections, Reichenbach thought frequencies to be accessible, and Popper thought propensities to be legitimate, in a way that probabilities are not. In all cases, one tacit aim is to analytically reduce probability by means of necessary and sufficient, or identity, conditions.

On a subjective interpretation, partial degrees of belief may be measured by means of 'betting quotients'.[4] Suppose two people, X and Y, are to hold a bet about a certain proposition P regarding the future, or a possible future event E, and suppose that we are interested in finding out X's degree of belief that E will occur. The betting quotient q that X is prepared to offer Y on a certain stake S may then be established as follows. If E takes place, Y will pay X a utility (e.g. money) given by the product of the quotient and the stake (i.e. $U = q \times S$); if E does not take place, then X will pay Y the stake S. Y fixes the stake S, which can be positive or negative, and it is fixed after X reveals his or her betting quotient but ahead of the event. Since X does not know whether S is positive or negative, it is in X's interest to reveal his or her true degree of belief in E as accurately as possible. Otherwise X stands to lose utility if the stakes are chosen appropriately. If Y were to reveal the stake S ahead of the betting, it would allow X to adjust the quotient accordingly and profit an in principle inordinate amount. For suppose the stake is positive; then X simply chooses a very large quotient q – thus enjoying maximal utility in case E does actually take place, and losing out only S if E does not take place.

Consider, for a particular example, betting on whether Arsenal will win the Premier championship next year. Suppose the real chance stands at 40 per cent.

---

[4] See Ramsey (1926, section 3) and Gillies (2000, pp. 61 ff.). There are issues I gloss over in the text concerning whether degrees of belief are behavioural dispositions merely, or have some more substantive psychological reality. For the less controversial relation between odds and betting quotients, see Mellor (2005, p. 67).

Y is merely interested in making money out of X, but X is a knowledgeable fan and his true degree of belief reflects the chance. However, if Y reveals a positive stake, then it is in X's interest to raise his betting quotient q indefinitely – for in case Arsenal actually goes on to win, X would receive a large utility, and in case Arsenal does not win, X would lose only the small stake, which would be returned to Y (i.e. X in fact loses nothing). If Y reveals a negative stake S, then it is in X's interest to lower his betting quotient well below 40 per cent and close to 0 per cent – for in case Arsenal fails to win, X would lose close to nothing. In fact, nothing so far prevents q from being a negative number, and it would obviously be in X's interest at this stage to fix a large negative q, which again would guarantee an inordinate amount of positive utility ($q \times S$) in case Arsenal wins the championship, and the mere loss of the stake (i.e. zero loss) in case it does not. However, if Y does not reveal its stake ahead of X's declaring the betting quotient, then it is in X's interest to neither go above nor below his or her true estimate of the chance of E – which we have agreed in X's case is reflected as his or her degree of belief. Therefore, the structure of the betting scenario entails that necessarily q will reflect accurately his or her degree of belief regarding E's chances. And now we see that the assumption that X's degree of belief correctly reflects the chances is also otiose in the argument, since everything it takes for q to accurately represent X's degree of belief is that X's degree of belief tracks X's best estimate of the actual chance of Arsenal's winning the championship, not the fact that indeed the estimate is correct.

Betting quotients are thus manifestations of agents' degrees of belief, which in an operationalist sense (Gillies, 2000, p. 57) fix the latter by measuring the former. Yet, so far there has been no requirement that betting quotients obey the calculus of probabilities, and therefore it has not been shown that degrees of belief are probabilities, or that they interpret probabilities subjectively. To show this requires additional technical work, what is known as the Ramsey–De Finetti theorem (proved independently by Ramsey in 1926 and by De Finetti in 1931). The theorem establishes that degrees of belief are probabilities on pain of *incoherence*, where coherence does not amount to internal logical consistency, or any other a priori consideration, but is instead related to rationality constraints in betting scenarios, which requires some explication.

An agent's degrees of belief – and the betting quotients that they express – are defined to be coherent if and only if it is not possible to formulate a *Dutch book* against the agent in any conceivable betting scenario, where a Dutch book is a combination of bets that would make the agent lose utility no matter what happens in fact. It is then relatively straightforward to show that betting quotients – or the degrees of belief they measure or represent – must be probabilities if they are coherent. An argument from coherence to the effect that degrees of belief and betting quotients are probabilities is therefore known as a *Dutch Book argument*.

To prove the Ramsey–De Finetti theorem requires a prior definition of probability. I will follow here what is nowadays known as the definition of classical probability, first formulated by Kolmogorov (1933), but it must be noted that this definition is posterior in time to both Ramsey's and De Finetti's proofs of their theorem. The differences between the axiom systems that both Ramsey and De Finetti adopted and Kolmogorov's own axioms are not without significance, particularly as concerns the notion of conditional probability,[5] but let that not detain us here since the difference is not significant for our purposes. Let $\{E_1, E_2, \ldots, E_n\}$ be the set of events over which an agent's degrees of belief range; and let Ω be an event which occurs necessarily. The axioms of probability may be expressed as follows (Gillies, 2000, pp. 59ff.; Mellor, 2005, pp. 15ff.):

Axiom 1: $0 \leq P(E) \leq 1$, for any $P(E)$: In other words, all probabilities lie in the real unit number interval.

Axiom 2: $P(\Omega) = 1$: The tautologous proposition – the necessary or certain event – has probability one.

Axiom 3: If $\{E_1, E_2, \ldots, E_n\}$ are exhaustive and exclusive events, then $P(E_1) + P(E_2) + \ldots + P(E_n) = P(\Omega) = 1$. This is known as the addition law and is sometimes expressed equivalently as follows: If $\{E_1, E_2, \ldots, E_n\}$ is a set of exclusive (but not necessarily exhaustive) events, then $P(E_1 \vee E_2 \vee \ldots E_n) = P(E_1) + P(E_2) + \ldots + P(E_n)$.

Axiom 4: $P(E_1 \& E_2) = P(E_1 / E_2) \times P(E_2)$. This is sometimes known as the multiplication axiom, the axiom of conditional probability, or the ratio analysis of conditional probability, since it expresses the conditional probability of E_1 given E_2.[6]

The function P maps the set of events over which probabilities are defined onto the real unit interval and is a probability function or (for countable versions of the addition law) a probability measure. The Ramsey–De Finetti theorem then shows that betting quotients, if they are coherent (if they are such that a Dutch book cannot be made against them), necessarily obey the axioms of probability

---

[5] Kolmogorov essentially defines conditional probability by means of the ratio analysis, while both Ramsey and De Finetti presuppose that conditional probability is a primitive that admits no explicit definition and aim instead to characterize it axiomatically. See, for example, Gillies (2000, pp. 65ff.)

[6] The fourth axiom is sometimes written in the form of Bayes' theorem, $P(A/B) = \frac{P(B/A)P(A)}{P(B)}$, although strictly this is just a consequence. Bayes' theorem is relevant to the theory of confirmation, since it helps evaluate the probability of a theory in the light of evidence, in a process known as conditional updating, as $P(T/e) = \frac{P(e/T)P(T)}{P(e)}$, as long as estimates are available for what are known as the priors, that is, the prior probability of the theory, $P(T)$, and the evidence, $P(e)$. See, for instance, Howson and Urbach (2006).

(i.e. they are probabilities). It follows that probabilities are at least potentially representations of partial degrees of belief (also known as credences), whether or not actually manifested as betting quotients. Hence, the theorem also shows that probabilities may be interpreted subjectively as credences.

The proof of the Ramsey–De Finetti theorem goes in four stages, corresponding to each of the axioms of probability, and is too long to be reproduced here in full.[7] I will just illustrate the nature of the proof (and the theorem) by showing how it applies to the second theorem concerning the certain event Ω. All betting quotients on a certain event must be one if they are to be coherent. The reason is provided by the following Dutch book reductio argument. Suppose a betting quotient q on Ω is greater than one. Then Y will always win by choosing a negative stake, S, since in that case X receives with certainty the utility $q \times -S > -S$; that is, X must give Y the utility corresponding to a quantity strictly larger than $|S|$. On the other hand, if X's betting quotient in Ω is less than one, then Y will always win by choosing a positive stake S, since in that case X receives with certainty the utility $q \times S < S$, which is less than the stake. The only way to avoid a Dutch book is for X to choose his or her betting quotient q to be one (i.e. $q = 1$). The same type of reasoning is easily generalizable to cover the remaining axioms. Coherent betting quotients must obey the axioms of probability; in other words, rational credences are in fact probabilities.

The subjective interpretation of probability is not, however, without its problems. Here I will only point out one, show how it has already made a tacit appearance in our reasoning so far, and provide some additional grounds for worry. The problem is this: in order to make the subjective interpretation of probabilities as credences work, we need to assume that not all probabilities are subjective or that at any rate some probabilities capture or describe objective matters of fact in the world. This points out nothing historically new, since we know from the historical scholarship that we reviewed in the Section 1 that probability is Janus-faced, or essentially dual. But it comes as a blow to accounts of probability that reduce it to credence or subjective partial degree of belief.

My point here is also different to the usual point that there are as a matter of fact objective probabilities that subjectivists cannot account for, such as the objective probabilities predicted by quantum mechanics.[8] My argument does

---

[7] The full version may be found in Ramsey (1926, section 3), Gillies (2000, pp. 58–64), or Mellor (2005, pp. 69–70).

[8] At any rate I am amongst those who believe it to be the case that there are objective as well as subjective probabilities. But then again, so is Ramsey, who in 1926 already pre-empted Carnap's (1950) dual concept of probability: 'Probability is of fundamental importance not only in logic but also in statistical and physical science, and we cannot be sure beforehand that the most useful interpretation of it in logic will be appropriate in physics also. Indeed the general difference of

not turn on the factual existence of objective probabilities. The argument is rather that the consistency of the subjective interpretation ultimately requires the recognition of an objective dimension to probability, or a representation of chances along with those subjective degrees of belief. This is in line with the claim that the duality of probability unearthed by the archaeological scholarship is present in contemporary philosophical discussions regarding the interpretation.

The appeal to objective probability was of course already present in the discussion of how an agent's betting quotients track or represent his or her degrees of belief. The argument implicitly appealed to the best estimation of chances, say the chance of Arsenal winning the premier league. Now, the reality of the chances themselves is not required by the argument since, as we saw, that assumption can ultimately be abandoned without loss of generality. What feeds into the argument is not the actual chance that Arsenal will win, but the best estimate of the agent – and the link between credences and betting quotients follows merely from the estimate regardless of how biased it may be. But what are these estimates of? Betting quotients are, as we saw, representations of the agent's credences – about what? A reasonable answer, shared by different approaches, is that they are best estimates of the underlying chances (the agent's best *estimate* of Arsenal's chance to win). If so, there is still implicit at the core of the subjective interpretation an assumption regarding objective chances.

Another way to put the argument is by considering the crucial notion of exchangeability in the subjective interpretation. According to reductionists, such as De Finetti (1937), or Savage (1954), exchangeability is an assumption required to reduce what appear to be objective probabilities to subjective ones. It supposes that any agent will ascribe the same probability to any sequence of events which exhibits the same frequency ratios of possible outcomes. Those sequences are then said to be exchangeable. De Finetti proved a theorem to the effect that such exchangeable sequences are to all extents and purposes indistinguishable from sequences of causally independent outcomes, that is, they satisfy a basic requirement of independence (see also Savage, 1954, p. 50ff). Thus, in the simple case of coin tossing, this amounts to the assumption that any sequence 'HTHTHTHT' is as probable as any sequence 'HHTTHHTT' since the ratio of heads to tails is ½ in both cases. If so, according to the definition any infinite sequence generated by the tossing of the coin 'HTTTHHTH ... ' is exchangeable. More generally, we say that an infinite sequence of random

opinion between statisticians who for the most part adopt the frequency theory of probability and logicians who mostly reject it renders it likely that the two schools are really discussing different things, and that the word "probability" is used by logicians in one sense and by statisticians in another' (Ramsey, 1926, p. 157).

variables $\{X_1, X_2, \ldots, X_n\}$ is *exchangeable* if for any finite cardinal number n and any two finite sequences $\{i_1, i_2, \ldots, i_n\}$ and $\{j_1, j_2, \ldots, j_n\}$, the two sequences $\{Xi_1, Xi_2, \ldots, Xi_n\}$ and $\{Xj_1, Xj_2, \ldots, Xj_n\}$ have the same joint probability distribution. De Finetti's thought is that the subjectively accessible property of exchangeability then may be used to reduce the objective notion of independence (or randomness) since his theorem guarantees that the latter follows from the former.

However, critics have argued that the theorem if anything shows the opposite, since independence is in fact presupposed in the very notion of identical joint probability distribution for randomly generated sequences. In other words, it is only under the assumption that the tosses are independent that exchangeability of any outcome sequence entails that any finite sequence will have an identical joint distribution. As Gillies puts it: '[. . . F]ar from our being able to reduce the notion of objective independence to that of exchangeability, the concept of exchangeability is actually parasitic on that of objective (causal) independence and so redundant. In order to use exchangeability in a way which does not lead to erroneous and misleading results, we have first to be sure that the situation is objectively one of independence' (Gillies, 2000, p. 77). The dual nature of probability thus seems to appear in the subjective interpretation too.

5 The Reality of Chance: Empiricism and Pragmatism

I have canvassed so far two interpretations of probability that emphasize and stress the epistemological (i.e. non-objective) side or dimension of probability. In their purest form each of these interpretations attempts to reduce the concept of probability to operative and manifestly epistemic concepts. The logical interpretation understands probability as a logical relation between propositions, such as partial degree of entailment or inductive support; the subjective interpretation understands probability as coherent partial degree of belief, or credence. In each case, the ultimate aim is to lay down necessary and sufficient conditions for probabilistic statements in terms of these epistemic properties. Occasionally, as we saw is the case with Ramsey, their proponents will accept that their theory can only account for the epistemic dimension or notion of probability, and that there is another objective or ontological dimension that remains untreated. But more often than not, the intent is ultimately reductive, and therefore implicitly dismissive of the reality of objective chance.[9]

---

[9] In some cases it is explicitly so, as when De Finetti writes (De Finetti, 2008, p. 43): 'Objectivist statisticians [. . .] reject the use of the initial probability because they reject the idea that probability depends on a state of information. However, by doing so, they distort everything: not only as they turn probability into an objective thing [. . .] but they go so far as to turn it into

This brief section is intended to offer some empirical instances of objective chances and hopefully will serve to strengthen the thought that the defender of subjective probability must at the very least offer some story to account for them. I then quickly run through some of the solutions that subjectivists have offered in response before I turn to a discussion of fully objective interpretations of probability.

Some of the games of chance that gave rise to the concept of probability in the seventeenth century on the face of it involve genuine operations on physically real chance set-ups yielding what look like undeniably objective chances – of the sort that cannot be rendered subjective. Consider dicing, where the physical properties of the die seem to minimally influence – if not fully determine – the probabilities for it landing on any of its different sides. Thus, a skewed, smaller, distorted, or otherwise defective side can lead to a very different, often much reduced, probability of the die falling on that side in the long run, and therefore to a higher probability of the number on that side appearing as the outcome. Similarly, a heavily biased coin, of greater density on one side than another, will in our common experience always lead to a different probability for heads and tails in the long run. These differences appear in our experience to be independent of any particular agent's degree of belief. They do not seem to depend on any agent's degrees of belief or state of knowledge, but solely on the actual physical constitution of the chance set-ups in question.

There are a multitude of similar examples across the natural and social sciences where the probabilities of particular chance set-ups or phenomena appear to be entirely independent of any agent's beliefs regarding them. A common example from physics is radioactive decay. One may helpfully summarize the main facts regarding radium decay as follows. Radium atoms have a chance p_t of decaying within t years. In the case of the most common isotope, radium-226, this is ½ in 1,600 years. To work out the chance of decay of a single atom in any single given period of time, we may employ the decay constant for exponential decay. Thus, radioactive materials exponentially decay in accordance to the formula $p_t = 1 - e^{\lambda t}$, where λ is the decay constant. The decay constant for Ra-226 is $\lambda = 1.4 \times 10^{-16}$ per second. Hence, the chance that an atom of Ra-226 would decay within a second is $p = e^{-1.4 \cdot 10^{-16}}$. Alternatively, a gram of Ra-226 will display on the order of 3.7×10^{10} decays each second (what is known as a *curie*). These sorts of numbers are constants for each kind of element and their isotopes. For example, less stable isotopes of radium will decay more quickly, in other words their probability of decay will

---

a theological entity: they pretend that the 'true' probability exists, outside ourselves, independently of a person's own judgement.'

be higher. Thus radium-228 has a half-life of 5.75 years, and radium-225 only 14.9 days. There is nothing subjective regarding these probabilities; it just simply seems wrong to think of them as measuring anyone's particular credence or degree of belief. Rather to the contrary, it would seem that anyone rational and informed should adjust their credences to these objective chances as far as possible. What can the subjectivist say in response?

There is a long history of attempts by subjectivists to either deny the reality of chance or to 'bring it under' the scope of subjective probability. For lack of space I shall not be able to fully assess these attempts here; but I would like mention just two of them. Firstly, we saw how De Finetti defended that the notion of exchangeability would be able to provide a subjectivist surrogate for the objective notion of probabilistic independence, and thereby provide a reduction of objective chance. Such an attempt was criticized above as misguided, but others in this tradition have attempted a reduction of a different kind. For instance, Hewitt and Savage (1955) generalize exchangeability to all random variables, and more recently Skyrms (1977) has suggested that resilience may do the trick (where a subjective probability is resilient roughly if it is no longer susceptible to major change or updating on the basis of new evidence, no matter what evidence may be forthcoming). The basic problems with these accounts are all in the spirit of the original objection to De Finetti's exchangeability surrogate: it is not clear in any of these cases that the accounts succeed except to the extent that they presuppose objective notions.

Secondly, there is the different 'Humean' tradition defended by David Lewis (1980), who claims to provide 'a subjectivist's guide to objective chance'. Lewis even advanced an influential *Principal Principle* that explicitly connects chance to credence. However, it is unclear whether this tradition in fact provides a subjectivist surrogate of objective chance, or rather an entirely different metaphysical conception of objective chance (as the sort of probabilities invoked by best system analysis statistical laws – see Hoefer (2018) and Ismael (2008; Forthcoming)). Thus, the role of David Lewis' Principal Principle is not necessarily one of grounding objective chance in subjective credence, but it is rather one of specifying and making explicit some of the functions that any metaphysical conception of objective chance must deliver (see Section 10 for further discussion).

I conclude that we have strong reasons to accept the reality of objective chance and that we are therefore in need of an account of the probabilities that ably represent objective chances across the sciences. The rest of the Element will deal with the question as to what these chances may be, or how they may be understood. Initially, in the next two sections, I shall address the philosophical issue head-on through the 'objective' interpretations of chance. In the second half of the Element (Sections 8–13) I enlarge the family of objectivist views considered and contrast the interpretational efforts with what I shall claim is a more promising approach in terms of modelling practice.

6 The Frequency Interpretation: Actual and Hypothetical Frequencies

Charles Sanders Santiago Peirce (1893, and many other writings) was probably the first philosopher to explicitly advocate and defend irreducible indeterminism in connection with chance phenomena. Peirce argued tirelessly against what he called 'the doctrine of necessity' (by which he meant, roughly, Laplace's determinism), and in favour of randomness and chance (Hacking 1990, ch. 23, Mayo 1996, ch. 12). Peirce's main inspiration was his practical work in geodetics at the US Coast Survey; he was amongst the first to argue for the legitimacy of statistical inference from data; to use sampling techniques as a foundation of inductive reasoning in general; and to argue first for a frequency theory of chance, and then later on in his life for a propensity account of probability. The frequency theory was first clearly stated in its modern form by John Venn (1866), and it went on to be developed fully by Richard von Mises (1928/ 1957) and Hans Reichenbach (1935/1949). Here I will mainly adopt and discuss von Mises' version. His account is squarely in the empiricist tradition, yet it is also objective because both the regularities and each of the involved facts are objective. In other words, this is a reductive account or, in Reichenbach's term, an 'identity conception' that identifies probability with frequency.[10]

The frequency account deals with chance as follows. The statement that the chance of decay of a Ra-226 atom within t years is p_t can be translated into a statement of frequency as follows: 'the frequency of radium-226 atoms decaying within t years is p_t'. Alternatively, if we fix on a curie, then 'in the large collection of Ra-226 atoms that make up one gram of this material the proportion of those that decay within a second is 3.7×10^{10}'. There are different ways of fleshing out this thought, but all of them share a commitment to probabilities understood as properties of groups, sets, or 'collectives' (in von Mises' phrase to be more closely studied later on). On the frequency view a single individual taken in isolation does not have any chances, or probabilities. Only groups or sets or classes of such individuals can be said to have chances. Statistical laws are called forth in those cases simply because there needs to be a reference to the whole collection of objects for a probability statement to make sense. Hugh Mellor (2005, p. 37) puts the point well when he writes: 'for frequentists there is no such thing as a chance p_t (other than 0 or 1) of a single

---

[10] See Howson and Urbach (2006, p. 50) for an alternative view on Von Mises' empiricism.

atom decaying in a given period of t years. Such a chance, in their view, is no more a property of a single atom than, for example, the property of being numerous is.'

von Mises (1928/1957) first introduced the notion of a 'collective' in order to ground frequencies, even in cases where there are no obvious explicit references to groups, sets, or classes of entities endowed with frequencies. The thought is that as long as a probability statement is meaningfully made, there must be implicit if not explicit reference to a collective, a sequence with a well-defined limit that remains invariant under place selection (von Mises' definition of a *random* sequence). But a collective is necessary because for any given event that is ascribed a probability, there must exist a whole family or class that this event is properly a part of. Suppose that I want to establish the probability that a particular atom will decay within an hour. The first thing I need to know is what kind of atom this is – the full description of the element and its corresponding isotope. But to be given this information is to be given implicitly a class that this particular atom is an instance or individual example of. The probability is then to be identified with some property that some of the elements in the class may have – a particular frequency. And this in turn is established as the ratio of the cases in the class that possess this property. If the probability of a radium-226 atom decaying in 1,600 years is ½, this means, on this view, nothing other than that exactly half of the atoms in this given class do decay within that specified period of time.

The proper definition of 'collective' is nevertheless plagued with difficulties, which ultimately make the frequency interpretation very difficult to maintain. von Mises introduced the notion of the attribute space Ω; this is the set of all possible outcomes of a particular repeatable trial, thus often also called the outcome space, over which probabilities are defined. The attribute space is constrained by both the population and the class of entities or properties relative to which the probability is defined. Thus, von Mises also distinguished empirical and mathematical collectives, and claimed that the latter were an abstraction or idealization of the former in the same way in which physics often abstracts away from concrete detail, thus focusing on idealized frictionless planes and so on (von Mises, 1928/57, pp. 99–100). Nevertheless, the strength of the analogy has often been disputed – for discussion see, for example, Gillies (2000, ch. 5). Yet without a mathematical notion of collective it is hard to see how the frequency definitions can be made to work, for all empirical collectives are finite, while probability distributions are continuous functions that map onto the full real number unit interval. On the other hand, the true empiricist commitment seems to lie with the empirical collectives, since these can be defined for the finite frequencies that we actually observe or record experimentally.

It is thus typical to distinguish between two different views: finite and hypothetical frequentism.[11] Finite frequentism is a slightly simplified version of the view defended by Venn and identifies a probability as applied to a particular finite population with the finite frequency ratio of a particular attribute or outcome in that population. Thus if, in a particular experimental run, I toss a coin exactly 50 times obtaining 22 heads and 28 tails, the probability of (the attribute) heads relative to the (collective made up of) 50 trials of this particular coin is exactly 0.44, and that of (the attribute) tails is 0.56. If I then go on to toss the same coin another 50 times obtaining 20 heads and 30 tails, the probability of (the attribute) heads relative to the entire (collective) of 100 trials is now 0.42 and that of tails is 0.58. And so on. It is clear that this conception satisfies the empiricist constraints that motivate frequency accounts of probability in the first place, but it is also clear that it makes probability a perilously ephemeral property of the particular finite empirical collective at hand.

There is a clear sense in which our ascriptions of probability, particularly in scientific domains, transcend such empirical collectives. For instance, the chance of a radium-226 atom to decay does not seem relative to – or in any other way constrained by – any particular empirical finite trial or observation of any particular sample of Ra-226. On the contrary, it is a theoretical result that appears at least in principle to be derivable from the quantum mechanical description of the stability of the atomic nucleus, and it is therefore independent of any particular trial on any particular sample. Similarly, we are tempted to think that the probability of a coin to land heads is an intrinsic feature of the coin in its proper context (which includes the features of the particular toss): it thus depends on the geometrical and physical properties of the coin together with the set-up and the particular circumstances involved in tossing it. The finite frequency account of probability denies this, and in so doing it appears to do some violence to our intuitions in these cases.

The finite frequency interpretation defines probability relative to an empirical collective. The main role of the collective is to lay down what is known as a reference class for the probability in question – this is the class of all the relevant events of the same type. The types may differ greatly depending on the level of description – as a result the probabilities too will differ, in ways that again seem contrary to our intuitions regarding the unconditional probabilities at stake. For example, the probability that I may develop lung cancer in the next thirty years is different depending on the collective that it is defined relative to, because the event of my developing lung cancer in the next thirty years belongs

---

[11] Mellor (2005, ch. 3) more finely distinguishes three views: finite, limiting, and hypothetical frequentism. I follow here more common use in lumping the limiting and hypothetical versions together – as in, for example, Hájek (2009).

to many different reference classes with different relative frequencies of positive outcomes to total number of cases. Thus, this probability is different if I am just regarded as a Western European, or a non-smoking male, or a person who regularly exercises, or who follows some healthy diet. This is sometimes known as the *reference class problem*. According to the finite frequency account, there is not in fact a probability that corresponds to this event, only an indefinite number of relative or conditional probabilities.

Hypothetical frequentism is often consequently advanced in order to overcome some of these difficulties. Instead of defining probability relative to a particular empirical collective, it defines it relative to the limit in the corresponding infinite collective; and it assumes that the limit coincides for all those empirical collectives that are sub-classes of this more general one. In other words, an infinite or mathematical collective must be selected *ab initio*. Thus, in my examples, all experimental observations on radium-226 atoms yield empirical collectives that have the appropriate limiting frequencies corresponding to the theoretical chance for decay. And the coin in the long term also tends to a particular limiting frequency (0.5 in the case of an unbiased coin), so both empirical collectives referred to above share the same limiting frequency even though their finite frequency ratios differ. This limiting frequency is guaranteed by the so-called axiom of convergence (von Mises, 1928/1957; see also Gillies, 2000, pp. 96ff.), which states that for any arbitrary attribute A of any collective C, then $\lim_{n\to\infty} m(A)/n(B) = p_c(A)$, where $P_c(A)$ is the probability of A in the collective C, or relative to its reference class.

Although the move to the hypothetical limit lets frequentism off the hook regarding empirical collectives, it creates a number of hard problems of its own, and unfortunately retains some of the deficiencies of the finite frequency analysis anyway. Let me here review just three of them. Firstly, notice that going hypothetical entails a surreptitious abandonment of the empiricism that motivated the frequency interpretation in the first instance. For the consideration of the limit brings with it not just a hypothetical situation (the running of an experimental trial an infinite number of times) but, most glaringly, an essential modal element that seems prima facie contrary to any empiricist strictures. What I have in mind is that the limit must be defined in relation to a counterfactual situation – one in which we toss the coin an indefinite number of times, under the assumption that the circumstances remain identical. In other words, we are asking not after the limiting character of an actual situation, but after a counterfactual limit in a counterfactual situation.

Take the example of a biased coin again. The hypothetical limit is that to which the outcomes of the coin toss would tend where the coin to be tossed under the same circumstances an indefinite (and potentially infinite) number of times. Assuming the circumstances stay the same (tossing on the surface of earth under the typical pressure level, in the same atmospheric conditions, on a surface of identical friction, with identical force, etc.), the probability of heads would be, say, 60 per cent, if that is the limit the frequency would tend to. However, nothing guarantees that the conditions would stay the same, and if pressure, friction, gravity, and other factors were to change, the limit itself would change, and so would, arguably, the probability. And, in fact, it is impossible to suppose that none of those circumstances would in the actual world change, however slightly, in a given period of time, however short. Therefore, in an infinite run, we may assume the conditions to change infinitely many times, and not necessarily slightly. To guarantee that the limit stays fixed, we need to guarantee the stability of the conditions, and this may only be achieved counterfactually.

Hence the hypothetical frequency account is not merely hypothetical, but counterfactual. It asserts that probability of a particular attribute A in a reference class R is the limit of the relative frequency of A's among the total number of cases in R that would be the case if there were an infinite sequence of trials under identical conditions, or infinite collective C. This is hardly fitting for an empiricist account of probability and seems to rob it of its main attraction – namely to provide an account of probability that does not resort to metaphysics.

The surreptitious abandonment of empiricism does not deliver the hypothetical frequency interpretation from all objections or difficulties anyway. The second main problem for the hypothetical frequency account is again a variant of the *reference class problem*. The definition of probability is on the hypothetical frequency account still relative to some reference class, however counterfactual or hypothetical. Thus, in the example of the coin above, the limit is defined relative to a particular collective, and therefore a reference class of similar tosses. The class is made up of a number of different events, and the decision which events to include or exclude may well determine whether the sequence of outcomes in the class has a limit and what this limit is. We may, for instance, choose to include all tosses with the same coin irrespective of all conditions – hypothetical or otherwise – that it is tossed in – that is, we choose to abstract away friction, gravity, and so on. Or we may choose to include all tosses with different coins of the same type on the same surface in the same gravitational field, and under otherwise identical experimental conditions. And so on. Each of these decisions will determine the nature of the infinite collective and its limiting frequency.

Finally, there are issues regarding the limiting character itself of hypothetical frequencies. It was noted that the axiom of convergence guarantees that there is a limiting frequency for every well-defined collective. Yet, the application of the axiom may be circular for the purposes at hand, and particularly so as part of a definition of probability as limiting frequency. One of the defining characteristics of a collective, according to von Mises, is a certain long-run stability of its attributes. Thus, the law of stability of statistical frequencies (von Mises, 1928/ 1957; see also Gillies, 2000, pp. 92ff.) guarantees that for any collective, a repetition of an experimental trial an indefinitely large number of times will eventually converge upon a particular number. While von Mises thought of this as an empirical law, it is also true that it is a law known to hold only for stable chance set-ups or arrangements that exhibit the sort of stability of properties required by the counterfactual condition discussed above. It is therefore implicitly a law that only applies to collectives. The application of the axiom of convergence is not valid for chance set-ups that are 'not stable' or for sequences of outcomes that are not properly part of collectives. In such cases, there is no guarantee that the sequence will have a limiting frequency for the attribute at hand, and therefore on a hypothetical frequency account there is no guarantee that there is any probability at all of the attribute in question (Hájek, 2009).

One final observation is that the resolution to these issues points again towards the dual nature of probability, as I have been stressing throughout the first half of this Element. The obvious way around some of these objections requires a judicious selection of chance set-ups and reference classes. On a frequency account of probability, ascriptions of probability to present events have a curious dependence upon future events – under a particular description. What kind of chance a particular attribute A now has in part depends upon the future frequency of A's within a relevant sequence. The sorts of problems involved are thus of a very similar sort to those regarding the projectability of 'entrenched' predicates in discussions of the problem of induction (Goodman, 1955), and the resolutions in practice correspondingly appeal to similar pragmatic judgements in both cases.

7 The Propensity Interpretation: Single Case and Long Run

The propensity interpretation of probability fully emerged in the 1960s as a realist attempt to overcome some of the difficulties with frequency accounts and to restore a robust objective interpretation of probability. Its historical sources, however, go a much longer way back to the end of the nineteenth century. Peirce defended a broadly dispositional account of probability, whereby dispositional properties inherent in chance systems and objects give rise to long-run stable frequencies. Critically, the dispositional properties according to Peirce reside in the very chancy objects themselves, who carry them over from situation to situation, regardless of hypothetical or counterfactual conditions. As he wrote (Peirce, 1910, p. 169) in relation to dice: '[. . .] the die has a certain "would-be"; and to say that a die has a "would-be" is to say that it has a property, quite analogous to any habit that a man might have . . . and just as it would be necessary in order to define a man's habit, to describe how it would lead him to behave and upon what sort of occasion – albeit this statement would by no means imply that the habit consists in the action – so to define the die's "would-be", it is necessary to say how it would lead the die to behave on an occasion that would bring out the full consequence of the "would-be"; and this statement will not of itself imply that the "would-be" of the die consists in such behaviour'.

The fundamental insight in this paragraph is, of course, the thought that probability is essentially a probabilistic disposition. Peirce went on to define the 'consequences' of this probabilistic dispositional property in accordance with his pragmatist maxim, which prescribes to think of any concept in terms of whatever manifestations or effects in thought the concept has in our mind. He noted that some or maybe all of those consequences would only be manifested in the long run. The actual long-run frequency that manifests the underlying disposition of a die is only revealed in the long term – in an indefinitely large sequence of trials of tossing the die. The pragmatist maxim has sometimes been confused with a version of the principle of verification so dear to logical empiricists. But note how unsuitable this is as a reading of Peirce's fundamental commitments. Under a verificationist reading the die's 'would-be' has no empirical consequences and is therefore meaningless. It follows, on this reading of the pragmatist maxim, that there are no probabilistic dispositions, which shows that this is the mistaken reading of Peirce's maxim. The version of the pragmatist maxim actually defended by Peirce does not stipulate that the manifestations or effects must be empirically accessible. Peirce's pragmatism is a historical antecedent of twentieth-century philosophy of science, but it was not a form of logical empiricism (and Peirce's own explicit diatribes against Hume make clear the extent to which he would want to distance himself from traditional empiricism, or more generally any foundationalist epistemology).

In other words, in accordance to the actual pragmatist maxim, for a concept to be well defined it matters not so much what the empirically accessible consequences are, as simply what the consequences in thought of the concept are, regardless of whether they are accessible or not. When it comes to probabilistic dispositions or chance, long-run frequencies in the infinite limit are fine as far as Peirce is concerned, as a clear and precise consequence or effect of chances. But they may not be identified with the chances themselves on pain of conflating cause and effect. The mere fact that we understand these frequencies to possibly display or manifest the underlying probabilities shows that the concept of probability has a well-defined meaning in accordance with the pragmatist maxim.

The view is prescient, both in terms of the critical objections to the frequency conceptions, and in terms of the version of an alternative propensity interpretation that would make sense. Peirce was thoroughly committed to objective real chance – as we saw in the interluding Section 5 – yet he refrained from any overly simple or straightforward reduction. Unfortunately, his lessons were not always clearly heeded, and the influence of the von Mises–Reichenbach empiricist reductionist projects was deeply felt in ways that cannot always be considered constructive or felicitous, in the various attempts to develop a propensity account of probability.

The most celebrated and better known amongst such accounts is due to Karl Popper, who developed his 'propensity interpretation of probability' in the late 1950s and early 1960s. It is well known too that Popper developed his propensity interpretation in response to some paradoxes of quantum mechanics. In particular he claimed that the resolution of the two-slit experiment requires a propensity interpretation of the quantum probabilities: 'The interpretation of the two-slit experiment … ultimately led me to the propensity theory: it convinced me that probabilities must be "physically real" – that they must be physical propensities, abstract relational properties of the physical situation, like Newtonian forces, and "real", not only in the sense that they could influence the experimental results, but also in the sense that they could, under certain circumstances (coherence) interfere, i.e. interact, with one another' (Popper, 1957, p. 28).

Unlike Peirce, however, Popper did not associate such propensities with the chancy objects individually taken, but with entire experimental set-ups instead. He thus contended that the same chancy object placed in different environments, subjected to different gravitational forces, and so on, would not only display different long-run frequencies but actually is endowed with different propensities. For instance, a biased die tossed on the surface of the moon would not only exhibit different frequencies for the different outcomes but in fact properly and legitimately possesses different propensities. In other words, Popper conceived propensities as relational properties of chance set-ups, corresponding with the different displays of long-run frequencies in each case: '[Propensities] are relational properties of the experimental set-up. For example, the propensity ¼ is not a property of our loaded die. This can be seen at once if we consider that in a very weak gravitational field, the load will have very little effect – the propensity of throwing a 6 may decrease from ¼ to very nearly ⅙' (Popper, 1957, p. 68).

Popper was committed to a thesis that I have elsewhere referred to as 'the identity thesis', according to which probabilities are propensities, and vice versa (Suárez, 2013, pp. 65–6). The identity thesis is the analogue for propensities of Reichenbach's identity conception for frequencies. It is a reductionist commitment in the spirit of the logical empiricist philosophy that I have discussed in previous sections. Its adoption by Popper (who by many other lights was a leading critic of logical empiricism) signals another important difference between Popperian and Peircean accounts of chance and propensity. Popper mainly came up with an *interpretation* of probability; and in his works propensities' only role is to provide a semantics for probabilities. Thus, according to Popper, one may solve the paradoxes of quantum mechanics merely by providing the right philosophical interpretation (i.e. the right model, in the model theoretic sense) of quantum probabilities as propensities.

By contrast, Peirce saw real chances everywhere, in every branch of science, whether theoretical or experimental, and as we saw he defended the identification of propensities with explanatory properties of chancy systems that would explain the long-term behaviour under appropriate testing conditions. In other words, Peirce ascribed propensities an explanatory role, not an interpretational one, and he thought that this role was nearly universal across the sciences. There is a world of difference between the rather limited claim that propensities are a model for probability, and the claim that propensities are real dispositional properties of chancy objects that we may postulate in order to explain experimental frequencies. For a start, the explanatory claim leaves open any issues regarding the identity conditions or the truth-makers of statements regarding probability since it does not make the claim that probabilities are propensities, or that probability statements are made true by propensity facts. On the one hand this leaves more work to be done; on the other hand, it nicely keeps neutral in the debate regarding the interpretation of probability itself. It may be that if the logical, subjective, frequency, and (Popperian) propensity interpretations of probability do not apply, this is because there are at least cases where no interpretation at all is applicable. Perhaps probability is a plural notion admitting no single or simple interpretation. If so, Peirce's views have an advantage since they do not prejudge the issue. (For discussion and extension of Peirce's views see Fetzer (1993) and Suárez (2013).)

The one aspect that Popper and Peirce prima facie did agree upon was the putative link between propensities (whether as dispositional properties of entire set-ups or isolated chancy systems) and long-run frequencies. In their younger periods both thinkers understood this link to be constitutive: propensities are at least in part to be thought of in terms of their manifestations or consequences. A theory of propensities that so links them constitutionally to long-run frequencies is known as a *long-run propensity theory*. The difference with long-run or hypothetical frequency views is slim but significant: where the propensity theory thinks of probabilities as features of repeatable sets of conditions that give rise to stable long-run frequencies, the frequency theory conceives probabilities as long-run frequencies directly – that is, without any intermediary detour via any conditions or other properties of chance set-ups. While the latter is open to an actualist reading (at least in the finite case), the former is explicitly dispositional and modal – since the repeatable conditions are precisely those ones that would give rise to the same long-run frequencies but only if the experiment were to be repeated often enough.

Later in their lives, both Peirce and Popper moved closer to a *single-case propensity theory* instead. The key difference is that the single-case theory can make sense of single-case probabilities regardless of any repeatable conditions (or regardless of any reference class or collective as required in the frequency view). The reason is that the propensities are ascribed to the chancy objects (or, alternatively, the entire set-ups) but without implicit or explicit reference to any repeatable conditions or the ensuing long-run frequencies. Take the old coin toss example. A single-case propensity theory in the spirit of Peirce ascribes the probabilistic dispositions to the coin itself independently of any experimental set-up, repeatable conditions, or frequencies in any sequences. In fact, the coin may never be tossed at all and still possess the propensities in question. On a long-run propensity view, by contrast, the coin only possesses propensities inasmuch as it may generate particular long-run frequencies in certain indefinitely long sequences generated in specified identical repeatable conditions. So properly speaking, as in the frequency view, the long-run propensity theory ascribes no probabilities to single experimental trials that may display the chances of objects but can only be performed once. (See, e.g., Gillies (2000) and Hájek (2009) for more detailed discussion.)

Yet, single-case chances seem obviously real and legitimate, in ordinary parlance or in science. Consider either the examples of the coin toss or the radioactive atom: There seems to be no reason that would prevent us from ascribing single-case chances to those systems, and in fact we routinely do so when considering the probability of heads in the next toss, or the chance of decay in the next minute. The long-run propensity view is therefore only viable to the extent that it has some surrogate notion for single-case chances. Some defenders of the long-run propensity theory have appealed to subjective probabilities at this point in order to furnish the required chances (Gillies, 2000, pp. 119ff.). Thus, the claim is that the single-case chances that appear in those instances above are nothing but our credences, or best estimates regarding those chances in light of our present information. Here we see again how subjective elements creep into the objective interpretations or theories of probability. It seems that the hybrid nature of probability emerges one way or another in any attempt to develop a full and consistent understanding of objective probability.

To conclude, this first half of the Element reviewed the state-of-the-art debate regarding philosophical interpretations of probability, as it stands today. It cast a particular eye on the historical scholarship of the last forty or so years, which unearthed unsuspected depth and complexity to our contemporary notions of probability. The nature of probability is essentially dual since its inception, incorporating both subjective and objective dimensions, and this shows in the difficulties that philosophers have had to face up to in developing either fully subjective or fully objective interpretations of probability *tout court*. The history reviewed in the first half shows probability to be plural in at least two senses. First, there are paradigmatic subjective and objective type probabilities out there – and none can be reduced to the other. Second, any coherent philosophical analysis of either type of probability involves both subjective and objective considerations. Thus, new conceptual space opens up for a thorough discussion of the practice of statistical modelling, which is the object of the second half of the Element.

8 Interpreting and Applying Objective Probability

The second half of the Element addresses the nature of statistical modelling and its import for the philosophy of probability. It returns to some of the interpretations reviewed in Sections 6 and 7 but focusing much more narrowly on objective probabilities, which are of greatest interest in an analysis of the practice of statistical modelling. In other words, we leave behind the first kind of pluralism, distinguishing subjective from objective probability, and from now on shall deal only with objective probability, or chance, as it appears in science. (This does not mean that subjective judgements are excluded from the analysis, so the second kind of pluralism shall remain relevant.) And while the first half of the Element is essentially historical, this second half adopts an analytical tone, which is reflected in the brief review of frequency and propensity interpretations in Section 9. I first introduce, in this section, a distinction between two different approaches to chance, contrasting the interpretative projects reviewed earlier with a new project in the application of objective probability more relevant to the practice of modelling.

Philosophers of probability have discussed the issue of the reality of chance or objective probability extensively, yet as we noted in the first half of the Element, the discussion has often been framed as part of a debate or dispute about the ontology and epistemology of chance. Realists have tended to focus on issues of metaphysical constitution and semantic reference; anti-realists have been concerned with evidence and epistemic accessibility. Hence empiricist-minded philosophers of science have attempted to reduce objective probabilities, or chances, to frequencies, or ratios of observable outcomes in experimental sequences of events. By contrast, metaphysically minded philosophers have attempted to interpret chance in light of propensities or dispositional properties. In either case the assumption is that chance is an obscure – or at any rate contested – concept that must be defined in terms of other simpler, more fundamental, accessible, or substantive concepts. While chances are not supposed to be accessible, frequencies are meant to be directly accessible through observation. And while chances are not supposed to be real and fundamental, dispositional properties are understood to be genuine properties of chance set-ups. It makes sense from the perspective of this debate about the ontology and epistemology of chance to attempt to reduce chance – objective probability – to either frequency or propensity.

Nevertheless, as we already know from the first half of the Element, both the frequency and the propensity interpretations of objective probability are ultimately not viable. The former encounters insurmountable difficulties associated to the so-called reference class problem; while the latter confronts a family of problems related to the notorious Humphreys' paradox. In the next section of this Element I briefly review these conclusive arguments, with an eye not so much on history as on analytical precision. In addition, I present a further explanatory argument that cuts against both frequency and long-run propensity interpretations. Chances are employed in practice for explanatory purposes, in science and in ordinary life alike; but I shall argue that this explanatory function remains elusive on any interpretation of objective probability that identifies it with sequences of experimental outcomes, or their conditions. The conclusion of this section is that it is time to consider alternative philosophical projects in our understanding of objective probability going beyond the interpretative endeavour, and I concur with Deborah Mayo when she states (Mayo, 2018, p. 13) that 'discussions of statistical foundations tend to focus on how to interpret probability, and much less on the overarching question of how probability ought to be used in inference'.

In the remaining sections of the Element, I consequently explore a different philosophical approach, which focuses instead on the role that chance plays in scientific modelling practice. In a brief slogan I aim to shift philosophical attention from the 'metaphysics and epistemology of chance' towards the 'methodology of chance modelling'. In particular I shall argue that chance plays an essential explanatory role in that practice, which already militates against any reductive analysis. Section 10 outlines metaphysical pluralism as applied specifically to objective probability. I argue for a tripartite conception that keeps propensities, single-case chances, and actual frequencies distinct. Section 11 advances a pragmatic statistical modelling methodology grounded on the tripartite conception, which I refer to as the *complex nexus of chance* (CNC). Let it be noted outright that this methodological turn is not intended to foreclose any option in the ontology of chance, and it does not resolve epistemic worries or concerns, which are likely to endure. While realists may want to take the explanatory power of objective probability as further evidence in favour of the reality of chances, anti-realists will deny the inference from the explanatory power of the chance nexus to its reality, and I do not here pretend to resolve such quarrels. Rather, my more modest aim is to show that the epistemological debate goes under different terms in this new methodological arena. What I propose is a new take on the question over the nature of objective probability, one that starts from the standpoint of methodological practice, and which raises problems and issues of its own – including possibly new versions of the perennial debates in the ontology and epistemology of chance.

Indeed, the thesis running through this part of the Element is that new and interesting philosophical questions arise for a philosophical study of objective probability once this new methodological outlook is adopted. The focus is in particular on the role that dynamical equations play in statistical modelling, and I shall argue in Section 12 that all statistical modelling in the natural sciences can be placed on a spectrum that goes from purely deterministic to purely indeterministic ('stochastic') dynamics. Many models use a mixture of both, and the regular assumption that all statistical modelling must invoke a thoroughly stochastic dynamics is disproven by the fact that many statistical models for macroscopic phenomena assume underlying deterministic dynamics. In the distinguished tradition of the method of arbitrary functions, which originates in the writings of von Kries and Poincaré at the turn of the nineteenth century, the 'stochasticity' is brought about in an ingenious way by a deterministic dynamics (in the traditional, Newtonian sense) that evolves a probability distribution defined over initial micro-variables into a probability distribution over the relevant macro-variables. I call this kind of modelling purely probabilistic, since the probabilities that it prescribes do not originate in the dynamics in or by itself. In contrast, what I call purely stochastic modelling requires no initial probability distributions over any dynamical variables – the final probability distributions arise naturally out of the dynamics. Much of statistical modelling, I argue, is *impure*, that is, it is neither pure probabilistic nor pure stochastic, but rather a mixture of both, and thus lies somewhere along the spectrum.

The concluding Section 13 of the Element wraps things up by pointing out that the CNC is in some ways a trivial consequence of the application of general philosophical lessons regarding the modelling attitude or methodology in general to the particular case of statistical modelling. There is little mystery to chance – to the ways in which the chance nexus is employed in practice – beyond whatever mysteries lie in scientific modelling in science in general. If that seems an uninspiring philosophical attitude, let it be remembered that it takes to heart every lesson from the history of the emergence of probability, and the everlasting disputes in the interpretation of chance. The hope is that such disputes may take a different and more tractable form within the more fertile ground of the distinctions characteristic of modelling practice.

9 The Explanatory Argument and Ontology

In this section I review more formal aspects of the approaches canvassed in the first historical half of the Element. The philosophy of probability throughout the twentieth century has been centrally concerned with providing an appropriate semantics for objective statements of probability, or chance. This in turn has been seen as requiring a description of what the world may be like for such statements to be true. And such a description at the very least requires the provision of some ontology for chance, or more technically, a stipulation of the truth-makers for our probability statements – those things in the world (objects, properties, facts, events) in virtue of which our probability statements are true or false. There are two broad approaches to this question throughout the twentieth century, answering to a markedly empiricist school earlier on, and to more broadly realist leanings later on.

9.1 The Frequency Interpretation

The empiricist tradition, recall, in particular the logical empiricists, understood an appropriate semantics for probability statements to entail reductions to observable facts or events – ascertainable directly by inspection or observation. The most likely candidate for such reduction – in Laplacean fashion – takes the form of ratios of outcome types, or attributes, in regular series or successions of observable events in repeatable experiments. Thus, von Mises (1928/1957) and Reichenbach (1935/49) formulated empiricist interpretations of probability by insisting that the range of possible cases be observable outcomes in repeatable sequences of experimental trials. The *frequency interpretation of probability* takes the form of a conceptual identity along the lines of: *P(A) is the probability of outcome A if and only if there is an appropriate sequence S of outcomes such that P(A) is the frequency or ratio of outcomes of type A in S.*

I shall refer to this generic statement as the *frequency identity* of probability, following the terminology introduced in Section 6. Hence, for example, P (heads) = ½ is the probability of heads in a coin-tossing experiment if and only if the ratio of heads to tails in the appropriate sequence S is exactly ½. It is easy to see how the *frequency identity* would generalize to more complex discrete or continuous probability distributions over a larger set of possible outcomes (a larger 'outcome space'). Thus, a probability of some attribute in some population can easily be identified with a frequency ratio of the attribute in a representative sample of the population.

The strategy seems at first sight the most natural way to deliver us from any unverifiable metaphysical commitments – often understood to be the holy grail of any empiricist philosophy. A traditional goal of empiricism ever since Hume, if not before, has been to analytically reduce unverifiable statements about unobservable or inaccessible entities or matters of fact so as to 'transform' them into verifiable statements about observable, or at any rate accessible, matters of fact. The empiricist tradition has attempted such reductions on problematic concepts such as lawhood (often, as in Mill or Mackie, identified with nomological regularity or non-accidental generalization); causation (which at least since Hume has been thought to be reducible to regular continuous succession, or a projection thereof); psychological time and personhood, and so on. In the context of chance and probability this has often translated into a requirement to express probability statements as claims regarding series or sequences of events that can be verified if not in practice at least in principle, and the frequency interpretation seems to readily deliver on just such a requirement.

However, recall that the 'frequency interpretation' is not really one single interpretation but a family of interpretations, generated by diverse renditions of the frequency identity. More precisely, all frequency interpretations obey the *frequency identity* as expressed above, but they differ as to what they take to be the 'appropriate' sequences in its defining statement. Very generally, we may classify frequency interpretations into two families: the finite frequency (FF) and the hypothetical frequency (HF) interpretations. Roughly, finite frequencies are ratios of outcomes endowed with the given attribute (A) in the *actual* (and hence necessarily finite) frequencies of experimental outcomes of real experiments performed on chance systems or set-ups. The FF interpretations thus have the virtue of reducing probability to an empirically accessible quantity. Since most if not all frequency interpretations are motivated by empiricism, this is clearly perceived to be an advantage.

Nevertheless, FF interpretations have severe problems or deficiencies; I will recapitulate here only the two problems that are most relevant to my purposes – the reader can find a full list in Hájek (1997). First of all, it is clear that for any actual finite sequence, no matter how large, the ratio of the appropriate attribute can in fact diverge from the probability. One need not consider weird situations such as those described in Tom Stoppard's play *Rosencrantz and Guildenstern Are Dead* (Stoppard, 1969), in which the characters repeatedly toss a coin that increasingly unnervingly always falls on heads. For a coin toss, any given odd-numbered finite frequency will necessarily diverge, however minimally, from ½. And we all intuitively understand that it is perfectly *possible* for any frequency, no matter how large, to diverge (and even to diverge maximally, as in the weird *Rosencrantz and Guildenstern* scenario). This sense of 'possible divergence' is built into the very judgement of the probability of any event in a series, as long as any outcome event is genuinely independent of any other (i.e. in the coin case: as long as the outcome at each toss does not alter the probability of any outcome at any later toss).[12]

The capacity of any finite frequency to diverge from the probability it is intended to analytically reduce comes under a variety of names in the literature (for instance, Hoefer (2018) refers to it as 'frequency tolerance'). I shall refer to it here as 'frequency divergence', since for every finite frequency exhibited in a regular experimental trial, there are myriad ways in which it may diverge from the underlying probability it can at best approximate. Note that divergence is not always an actual fact but a capacity: a frequency has the capacity to diverge from the probability, even though for any given t, the frequency up to t may not have yet diverged. There are purposes in the study of frequencies for which frequency divergence comes in handy, such as in assessing or ranking the 'faithfulness' or 'representativeness' of possible frequencies in sequences. However, as regards the finite frequency version of the frequency identity, it is ultimately lethal. For if any finite frequencies can as a matter of principle diverge arbitrarily from the probabilities they are supposed to conceptually reduce, then the frequency identity is surely false: there can be no sequence S that exhibits the appropriate frequency with any certainty, and this would entail that there is not really a probability $P(A)$ of the attribute in question, contrary to the assumption (of divergence). Hence finite frequencies – while undeniably centrally involved in any epistemology of chance – do not analytically reduce probabilities. Or, conversely, probabilities are not finite frequencies, contrary to what strict empiricism requires.

---

[12] The expectation for identically independently distributed (IID) random variables is widespread, as is the further expectation, to be explored in the next few sections, that 'divergences' ought to be tolerated (i.e. assigned credences greater than zero).

9.2 The Propensity Interpretation

It was noted in Section 7 that a way to circumvent these objections is thus precisely to give up on the strict empiricist commitments and to adopt a realist interpretation of objective probability instead – in terms of propensities. Propensity interpretations themselves come in a considerable variety. For example, it is customary to distinguish *long-run* from *single-case* propensities. In a single-case version, the underlying propensity is manifested in every single run of the experiment as a probability $P(A)$. In the long-run version of the propensity interpretation, by contrast, the function $P(A)$ is rather identified with the long-run frequency – thus Gillies (2000, ch. 8) asserts the single-case probabilities can only be subjective if anything. One may then substitute a long-run *propensity identity* in place of the frequency identity roughly as follows: *P (A) is the probability of some event type A if and only if A is a possible outcome of a chance set-up S endowed with a certain propensity P (A) to generate outcome A in the long run.*

However, any propensity interpretation – of either variety – that adopts a strict identity between probabilities and propensities fails too for reasons that have been explored extensively in the literature (Eagle, 2004, Humphreys, 1985, Salmon, 1979, Suárez, 2013). First of all, it is well known that many well-defined objective probabilities cannot be identified with any propensities. In fact, many conditional probabilities that have a straightforward propensity interpretation also often have well-defined inverse conditional probabilities that fail to have any propensity interpretation. Salmon's (1979) original example involved shooting's propensity to kill, which precludes any interpretation of killing as a propensity to shoot. But one can think of myriad other examples: smoking has a certain propensity to produce lung cancer, while lung cancer does not have a propensity to generate smoking – yet, for any control population, if the conditional probability of lung cancer given smoking is well defined, so is the inverse conditional probability of smoking given lung cancer. And so on.

The underlying problem, recall, is that propensities exhibit an asymmetry akin to cause and effect, and this is an asymmetry lacking in probabilities. Any *propensity identity* that identifies the two will ensue in contradiction: this shows that they cannot be the same thing. Humphrey's paradox (Humphreys, 1985) provides the definitive objection, since it shows that many bona fide propensities are not interpretable as conditional probabilities, on pain of contradiction with the Kolmogorov classical calculus. While there are a number of possible resolutions to this 'paradox',[13] they all involve giving up the propensity identity

---

[13] See Berkovitz (2015) for a detailed exposition of ongoing attempts to overcome the paradox and retain the propensity identity. To my mind the best such attempt involves rejecting the

in some respect. As has been shown already, the best rendition of propensities is not as an identity or analytical reduction of any sort for probability. Thus a defensible statement relates propensities to probabilities for outcomes in experimental trials or set-ups, but it does not identify them: *P (A) is the objective probability or chance of outcome A if and only if A is produced by a chance set-up S endowed with a certain propensity to generate each A with some probability P (A)*. In this statement, a propensity is ascribed to a set-up when an objective probability obtains for some outcome of that set-up – yet the propensity and the probability are not identified, but rather kept entirely distinct.

We may conclude that the propensity identity is a flawed but necessary presupposition in a long-run version of the propensity interpretation. It is also commonly adopted for single-case versions, but it does not turn out to be in fact necessary. On the contrary, as has been pointed out (Mellor, 2005; Suárez, 2013), there is a kind of single-case propensity that does not entail or require any identification with probability, and it is the notion adopted in the remaining sections of this Element, particularly Section 10.

9.3 The Explanatory Argument

I now turn to a different argument against any analytical reduction of probability by means of any identity thesis. It is related to the explanatory power of chances or objective probabilities – so we may refer to it as the 'explanatory argument'. This argument will provide the basis for the discussion of statistical modelling practice in the remainder of the Element. The point is best made in the context of attempts to reduce probability to frequency by means of the frequency identity (although it applies to a 'propensity identity' too). Objective probabilities in practice often explain regular occurrences of types of outcomes in different kinds of sequences. For instance, we explain the relative frequencies of a game of roulette, or dice, in virtue of the chances that are presumably operative in the game in question. If you ask me why I got 5 heads and 5 tails in tossing a coin, I can legitimately offer the explanation that it is a fair coin – that it is built so as to display such a probability. More generally, science will often invoke theoretically grounded probabilities in the

---

Kolmogorov axioms in favour of an altogether different formal axiomatization of probability, such as the one in Renyi (1955). Such alternative axiomatizations have not caught on, but recent critiques of the ratio definition involved in the fourth Kolmogorov axiom independently support them (Hájek, 2003), so the issue remains intriguingly open. At any rate, the rejection of the propensity identity does not invalidate the concept of propensity per se. On the contrary, as I argue in the following sections, propensities are an essential part of objective probability. However, their role is explanatory rather than interpretational, which does not sit in well with the identification of propensity with probability anyway.

explanation of observed frequencies. The difference between the observed decay rates of two pieces of radioactive material may be explained by reference to their half-lives, which are consequences of their different atomic structures. The difference between the recovery rates of two sorts of patient afflicted by the same condition may be explained by reference to the efficiency of the different kinds of treatment they have been subjected to, and so on.

This is a basic explanatory fact, which I will at this point in the argument take as primitive: probabilities are often invoked and used – in ordinary cognition and scientific practice alike – in order to explain frequencies. Yet, if the FF interpretation is correct, probabilities are frequencies, and it is impossible for a frequency to explain itself. It may be objected that the frequency explained is not the frequency involved in the explanation, so that the situation is not as blatantly circular as it may at first seem. As we shall see, this is essentially the response adopted by sophisticated Humean accounts, such as Hoefer (2018): perhaps not all frequencies are explanatorily on a par. Yet as long as we restrict ourselves to finite frequencies (as the FF interpretations do), it is very hard to see what the explanatory power of some frequencies over others could be. They are, after all, just the same *kind* of thing, and explanatory power requires some distinct property to be doing the explaining. It cannot serve to explain the actual finite frequency ratio in a chancy experiment to merely point out to another actual finite frequency ratio in that experiment: to do so would seem to merely expand the demand for explanation.

The issue may have less to do with circularity than with the weakness of the explanations provided by frequencies in any case. The larger actual frequency does not seem to add much from a robustly explanatory point of view. In other words, it may be thought at this point that the problem lies with the *finiteness* of the frequencies. As noted in Section 6, finite frequencies (FF) may be expanded into hypothetical frequencies (HF). An HF interpretation identifies probabilities with hypothetical frequencies over ideal infinite sequences of experimental outcomes that contain the appropriate finite subsequences whose properties are to be explained. For instance, in the case of a tossing coin, the appropriate frequency that identifies the objective probability or chance is supposed to be only definable in the abstract as the limiting frequency of the hypothetical infinite sequence of tosses. Presumably, if the coin is fair, the limiting frequency in the hypothetical infinite sequence is precisely ½. This may answer the first objection from frequency divergence in Section 9.1, since any finite frequency is allowed to diverge from the much larger (hypothetical and infinite) frequency. The large number theorem shows that the degree of divergence is inversely proportional to the length of the sequence, or in other words the finite frequencies will approach the limiting frequency as the finite sequence grows – and the finite frequency will become the actual probability in the infinite limit. However, that is just another way to concede that for any finite frequency, no matter how large, there can always be a degree of divergence.

The move to HF interpretations is not really successful in resolving the problems generated by the reference class problem, and in fact raises additional and important difficulties. There are at least two reasons why HF interpretations fail. First of all, for any given finite frequency there is a large number of consistent hypothetical frequencies, since for any finite subsequence, there are a large number of sequences that would include the subsequence as their initial segment. The large number theorem is no retort, since it presupposes that there is an actual probability and then goes on to show that the limiting frequency will arbitrarily approach it. However, the point of a frequency interpretation of probability is not to *presuppose* the existence of an actual probability that frequencies can be shown to approach in the infinite limit. The point of a frequency interpretation is to *identify* the probability itself *as the frequency* in accordance with the *frequency identity* discussed above. In other words, the large number theorem cannot really help to define probabilities as limiting frequencies in hypothetical sequences – rather the theorem only works on the assumption that there are probabilities independent of any frequencies or their limiting character.

At any rate, the explanatory argument remains; for the explanatory power of a frequency in a *hypothetical* sequence remains elusive. (A similar argument applies to long-run propensities.) On the one hand, if the explanatory power relies on merely subsuming the finite sequences whose frequencies are to be explained within the hypothetical sequences that putatively explain them, we have the recurrent problem above with FF interpretations: we seem to have merely expanded the demand for explanation. If, on the other hand, the appeal is to antecedent explanatory probabilities, as in the large number theorem, we restore the explanatory power but at the expense of postulating probabilities over and above any frequencies, or long-run propensities. What does the explanatory work in all these cases are facts that go beyond frequencies and long-run propensities. The explanatory power rather derives from the objective chances that frequencies may only be said to approximate in some limit.

10 Metaphysical Pluralism: The Tripartite Conception

The first half of the Element provided a lengthy argument for the limitations of any reductionist project. It suggested instead to adopt pluralism regarding probability. Rudolf Carnap (1945), Frank Ramsey (1926), and Ian Hacking (1975), amongst others, already argued that we must carefully distinguish objective probability (chance) from subjective probability (credence, or partial logical entailment). Carnap, moreover, argued that the conflation of these forms of probability leads to contradictions, confusions, and / or paradoxes, which only the correct formal explication of the concept is able to resolve. Ramsey and Hacking did not explicitly embrace such hopes of coexistence, but all their views are united in the rejection of the view that there is one single thing that probability is – or measures. Thus, all these authors emphasize distinct uses and historical origins in subjective and objective probabilities[14]. This is not yet pluralism about chance or objective probability, but it suggests that such a pluralism is one natural step on the road – and pluralism about specifically objective probability is exactly what I shall be urging in this section.

Earlier, in Section 8, I distinguished two kinds of pluralism. The first kind of pluralism, recall, invites the thought that there are different types of probability, and urges that the term 'probability' is in need of disambiguation. Carnap distinguished probability$_1$ and probability$_2$, and the distinction between credences and chances is nowadays entrenched. To go further down the pluralist road in this sense involves acknowledging that each type of probability may be further subdivided. Carnap's terms 'probability$_1$' (or 'subjective probability', or 'credence'), and 'probability$_2$' (or 'objective probability', or 'chance') may themselves require disambiguation in just the same way.[15] Thus, I shall suggest that objective probability ('probability$_2$') can be further subdivided into three different categories that are mutually irreducible (including pairwise combinations of the other two), namely 'propensity', 'single-case chance', and 'frequency'. Our conceptual repertoire contains the relevant notions, and it is sensible, in light of the discussions reviewed earlier in the Element, to countenance the corresponding metaphysical distinctions.[16]

The tripartite distinction then orders the different notions in a natural explanatory order. The propensities of the systems investigated – which, recall, on this view are dispositional properties of simple or composite complex systems taken on their own – when placed within sufficiently stable chance set-ups give rise to, or ground, an array of single-case chances that manifest such

---

[14] This undeniably glosses over the important differences on other grounds that exist between Ramsey's, Carnap's, and Hacking's accounts of probability.

[15] My focus here is on objective probability, so I have nothing to say about whatever ambiguities are involved in 'subjective probability'. But note that a similar disambiguation is plausible between betting quotients, descriptive degrees of belief, and normative or ideal credences of the sort that characterize objective Bayesian approaches (Williamson, 2010).

[16] See Suárez (2013, 2017a, 2018). These papers represent roughly an application of the sort of transcendental argument characteristic of naturalistic metaphysics (Cartwright, 1999, pp. 23ff.). Thus, I let well-established conceptual divisions – as they emerge in our cognitive practice – guide the metaphysical distinctions we draw in nature, as opposed to, conversely, attempting to build conceptual distinctions upon some prior metaphysics.

propensities.[17] There is a sense in which the dispositional properties naturally explain the single-case chances that emerge within each context, but it is important to note that the possession conditions of propensities are not in turn also sufficient conditions for the manifestations: Each system – whether simple or composite – can and typically will manifest different chances when placed in different set-ups. The propensities 'carry with them' this plethora of possible manifestations.[18]

In a further step, the single-case chances so established are then employed in order to explain a range of observed data, and in particular the frequencies exhibited by certain related attributes in the modelled data. This explanation typically takes the form of an embedding of the frequencies within the chance functions, either by showing that the 'surface' or experimental probabilities in the data models coincide with the chance functions for the elements in the range sets of both functions; or, in the case of finite frequency data, by embedding those discrete frequencies within the continuous distributions in the chance functions.

The tripartite distinction may be illustrated by some epidemiological models of contemporary currency. Models of infectious diseases, such as the SIR (Susceptible-Infectious-Recovered) model due to Kermack and McKendrick (1927) postulate a number of chances, such as the infectivity rate of an individual at a particular stage in the development of his or her disease (ϕ_θ). While this variable mainly depends on biological properties (the physiology of the individual, as well as the characteristics of the infectious agent), it is manifested differently (i.e. takes different values) depending on environmental factors, such as the average mobility of the individuals, the density of the populations they interact with, as well as particular environmental circumstances that may affect it, such as atmospheric pressure, weather, presence of antigens or other pathogens that may interfere with the course of the infection, and so on. For each of these sets of environmental conditions, the same physiology and infectious agent can result in greatly varying infectivity rates. Moreover, Kermack and McKendrick (1927, p. 718) show that when the ratio of susceptible to recovered in the population is close to the threshold value for herd immunity, very slight changes in infectivity rates can lead to dramatic differences in the

---

[17] The term 'manifestation' is here employed in the dispositional sense of Mellor (2005) and Suárez (2013), and it involves no requirement that the single-case chances be observable or in any way directly ascertainable by the senses.

[18] This thought may be cashed out either in terms of conditionals made true by the possession conditions of the propensities, or in terms of realist ascriptions of multiple properties encoded in each propensity. At any rate the relation between the propensities and their manifestations is not prima facie – or not always – one of simple cause and effect, but is best understood as multiple partial causation, or even a species of grounding. For further elaboration, see Suárez (2018).

course of the epidemic. Obviously in any practical application of epidemiological models, all these variables are then tested against the time-evolving frequency ratios of 'susceptibles', 'infectives', and 'recovereds' in the observed population (Kucharski, 2020).

I shall return to the representation of the diverse variables within the SIR model in Section 11; what is relevant here is that there are three distinct notions at play in these models, which reflect the tripartite categories of propensities (i.e. the dispositional properties of organisms and infectious agents), single-case chances (probabilities of infection, or transmissibility of the pathogen that the propensities of organisms give rise to within particular environmental conditions), and frequencies (of observable dynamical attributes within the population as the infection spreads). Thus, our practice vindicates a metaphysical pluralism about objective probability itself; it is not only impossible to reduce single-case chances to propensities or frequencies (or vice versa), but the three notions play a distinct and identifiable role within statistical modelling practice.

In Section 8 I noted that a second kind of pluralism will in addition remain significant, namely, there are a number of 'subjective' considerations that come into the determination of objective probabilities. Some of the 'subjective' judgements involved in applying the tripartite conception in statistical modelling of the phenomena shall be discussed in the next section. I end this section commenting on several subjective considerations which, in a more robust way, may come into the very notion of chance involved in the tripartite conception.

First, note that the truth-makers of statements involving each of the notions in the tripartite conception are suitably distinct. Statements about propensities are made true by the properties ascribed to the systems of interest (even if identifying and isolating the 'system of interest' is no trivial matter – as we shall see in Section 11). Statements of frequencies are, on this account, made true rather simply by the proportions of items with a given attribute within a sequence (even if the selection of the 'sequence' is also driven by data modelling). But what are the truth-makers of single-case chance statements? There are several proposals in the literature, and the point of the tripartite conception is not so much to avoid discussion of the nature of chance as to attempt to regiment it better. Thus, earlier I pointed out that my tripartite pluralism is compatible with a no-theory theory of such chances, such as Sober's (2010), according to which there are no truth-makers for chance statements beyond their assertion conditions within models. Yet, there are also some more substantive proposals, which help somewhat to understand the explanatory role that chances play in practice, such as Nina Emery's (2017), which grounds the nature of chance as nomological probability upon modelling and theorizing methodology. A similar account is Lyon's (2011), who countenances what he calls counterfactual probability as a distinct form of objective probability, beyond 'primitive' propensity. As we shall see in Section 11, 'subjective' elements come into the judgements routinely employed in such methodologies, so there is an element of subjectivism in this account too – even if the truth-makers of chance statements on this account are whatever nomological posits make them true.

Finally, there are extant philosophical accounts of chance that bring in subjective notions in a more robust manner as part of the very definition of chance. One such account, already noted, is Skyrms (1977), which proposes to analyse chances (from our point of view confusingly referred to as 'propensities') as robust or resilient subjective probabilities. More recently, there have been attempts – in the tradition of Lewis (1980) – to derive 'Humean' objective chances (HOC) as the posits of the best system analysis of space-time coincidences and their regularities (Loewer, 2004; Hoefer, 2018; Ismael, 2008; Forthcoming). In Hoefer's (2018) version, chances are the representations of all actual frequencies in the strongest, fittest, and simplest theory of what he calls *stochastic nomological machines*, the sorts of set-ups endowed with propensities that give rise to stable single-case chances, in our terminology.[19] Since there are pragmatic judgements involved in the assessment of strength, simplicity, and fit – not to mention their best balance – the nature of chance itself is subjective and relies on such pragmatic judgements. Yet, the theory has the advantage that it gets around the explanatory argument I developed in Section 9.3. The chances explain the finite frequencies that we observe simply by embedding the sequences these frequencies belong to within the larger (indefinite, if not infinite) regularities that make up the chances in the best system theory.

Any of the accounts of single-case chances that I have here described (Sober's deflationary, Emery's nomological, Lyon's counterfactual, Skyrm's resilient, or Hoefer's Humean objective chances) is compatible with the tripartite conception, and I do not wish to insist on any one of them in particular. It is even possible, and in line with the pluralism that guides this Element, that each of them describes one way in which some chances are. What all these accounts have in common is their emphasis on the explanatory role that chance plays *vis a vis* frequencies within statistical modelling methodology, and that is the subject of the next section in this Element.

---

[19] Hoefer is here following Cartwright (1999), whose non-Humeanism inspires my account too.

11 Methodological Pragmatism: The Complex Nexus of Chance

In scientific modelling practice, chance appears in a nexus of properties that typically includes probabilistic dispositions or propensities (represented by certain parametrizations of the phenomena); single-case chances (represented as the model's formal probability distribution functions); and frequencies in actual or imagined data (represented as limiting ratios, or 'surface probabilities' within models of data). The *complex nexus of chance* (CNC) is the set of interrelations between these three distinct notions in modelling practice. In adopting the terminology of 'propensities' as the dispositional properties of chance set-ups that ground probabilities (Suárez, 2018), my view moves decisively away from long-run propensity theories that ultimately identify propensities with either finite, infinite, or hypothetical frequencies. In distinguishing the formal probability functions that represent single-case chances from either propensities or frequencies, any interpretational identification of the former in terms of the latter is precluded. Finally, in emphasizing the role of finite experimental frequency data, the nexus of chance retains an empiricist outlook, which justifies probability statements empirically in terms of their relation to the actual data collected in genuine experimental and observational contexts (broadly in agreement with a long tradition including Suppes (1962), Van Fraassen (1993), and Mayo (1996, 2018)). On this view the only genuine frequencies are proportions or ratios of outcome types within the actual sequences of experimental outcome events; any limiting or hypothetical frequencies will appear only as extrapolations within models.

One of the immediate consequences of the view is that propensities are not automated interpretations of chance functions, but rather the sorts of properties of chancy systems that give rise to those chances; hence they are postulated or hypothesized as part of the CNC, since they appear as prepared descriptions of the phenomena. It follows that, like with any other theoretical postulate, propensity ascriptions are subject to empirical testing. We test them typically indirectly via the chance functions they generate in particular experimental contexts; but we also have plenty of knowledge about the mechanisms that may be operative and routinely probe into those background assumptions by the usual means: checking for their compatibility and overall coherence with other assumptions – in other words, their prior plausibility in light of other knowledge we possess.[20]

---

[20] Hence, we can apply the theory of confirmation, and in particular Bayes' theorem (see Section 4), to these assumptions in order to assess the weight that evidence has on them. That is, we estimate subjective prior probabilities for the assumptions ($P(T)$), and the evidence ($P(e)$), calculate the

While the tripartite conception has been defended already at a theoretical level, the nexus of chance remains to be studied at the level of modelling practice. The last three sections of this Element are an attempt to establish a philosophical research programme into the workings and operations of the CNC in modelling practice. Note that statistical modelling involves not merely formal descriptions of correlation phenomena; it is rather typically employed with explanatory purposes. In other words, the typical explananda are already prepared descriptions of statistical correlation phenomena between a set of interrelated 'observable' variables – which may indeed be observational variables in a data model, but may also represent properties of an underlying phenomenon in a controlled experiment, or the results of various interventions carried out in laboratory conditions. The basic explanatory tool in chance explanations of such statistical phenomena is a model featuring probabilities evolving in accordance to some dynamical law. In other words, the chances that figure in the propensity models are the putative explanans for the frequencies that appear in the data models and stand as the explanandum. If so, the explanatory relation is essentially one between two different types of models.

Thus, the probabilistic models deserve some attention. A common assumption in the philosophical literature is to suppose that a *probability model* is simply a probability or chance distribution function defined over the observable variables. To take the common – and apparently most simple – illustration of the coin toss: if a coin is tossed repeatedly, under identical conditions, the series of outcomes would constitute the observable data. Suppose the finite data exhibits a 47 per cent incidence of heads and a 53 per cent incidence of tails. A *probability model* is then, in accordance to this common view, an ascription of a probability distribution that can account for, or make sense of, this distribution. It is obvious that a 47–53 per cent probability distribution is the one that best accounts for, and makes sense of, this distribution, but others may do too within acceptable margins of experimental and systematic error. (What 'acceptable' margins of error are is an eminently relevant question and the object of considerable debate – see Mayo (1996, 2018)).

I do not have any fundamental quarrel with this simple definition of a *probability model* – as long as it is clearly understood that it is not the same notion as the more sophisticated *statistical model* that statisticians and scientists

---

probability of the evidence in the light of these assumptions ($P(e/T)$), and thus arrive at relative values for the probability of the theoretical assumptions in light of the evidence ($P(T/e)$). The assumptions regarding propensities lead to the ascription of objective chances for particular happenings out of the systems we are investigating, so this Bayesian checking procedure is yet another instance of how subjective probabilities are involved in postulating any objective chances.

use in their everyday modelling practice. To illustrate the difference, it is worth considering again what the model of a fair coin would be. On the philosophical notion of a probability model, this could only be the ascription of a flat probability distribution ρ (i.e. equal 50–50 probabilities) over the head (h) and tail (t) outcome events: $\rho : \{h, t\} \rightarrow \{\frac{1}{2}\} \in \mathbb{R}$. But as we shall see in Section 12, the statistical model of the phenomenon of coin tossing, even for a fair coin, turns out to be a much more complex and interesting entity.

The SIR models in epidemiology that we discussed briefly in Section 10 provide another illustration. The nowadays much discussed basic reproducibility number of an epidemic, $\mathcal{R}_0$, is calculated after some 'statistical model' assumptions have been put in place, including those that lead to particular values of the critical objective chances at the basis of epidemiological predictions.[21] In any SIR model the population as a whole is divided cleanly into three mutually exclusive classes, those susceptible to infection (S); those already infected, and hence infective (I); and those recovered (R), who are no longer susceptible or infected. It is thus assumed that infection leads to permanent immunity; that the population mixes homogeneously, and that there is an objective chance τ for any infective on average to infect a susceptible person, on any given day, in a population where everyone else is susceptible. Then, the size of the population N (also assumed to be constant in time, so that deaths and births nicely cancel out) is just the sum of S + I + R, and if the daily average number of personal encounters of significant proximity for the transmission of the pathogen is n, then the total number of susceptible infected daily by this one infected person is $\beta = \tau n$. Another variable, ν, describes the chance of recovery of any infected person on a given day on average, and is similarly derived from a combination of physiological and biological factors regarding the pathogen's action in the human body and the standard duration of the infection. The basic reproducibility number, which must be kept below one for the epidemic to be contained, is then calculated as the ratio $\mathcal{R}_0 = \frac{\beta}{\nu}$ and is a dynamical variable, since both β, ν are. It may only be estimated within a 'statistical model' in light of a number of relatively strong assumptions regarding the propensities of the systems involved, and their dynamical evolution. (For the fascinating history of $\mathcal{R}_0$, see Heesterbeek (2002).)

Two critical differences between *probability* and *statistical* models emerge. First, in a statistical model there is not a single chance distribution function but a *parametrized family of functions*, in a sense to be specified. Second,

---

[21] See Kucharski (2020), which moreover describes the role of mechanical assumptions – regarding what I would argue are the underlying propensities – in the epidemiological modelling tradition inaugurated by Ross (1910), to which Kermack and McKendrick (1927) belong. For a recent summary of epidemiological models, see also Bird (forthcoming).

a statistical model is dynamical: the chance functions in a statistical model either evolve in time, or they may apply to different stages of a dynamical process. It is the conjunction of these two distinguishing features (multiple parametrization, dynamics) that endows a statistical model with explanatory power.

An influential article (McCullough, 2002, p. 1225) expresses the first feature as follows: 'A statistical model is *a set of probability distributions* on the sample space *s*' (my italics). That is, a statistical model requires an antecedent parametrization of the phenomenon: a typically dynamical description of the phenomenon under some set of parameters. It is only once the phenomena to be modelled is so described that a properly parametrized statistical model can be provided for it, by ascribing to each parameter a distinct probability function over the sample space: 'A parametrized statistical model is a parameter set Θ *together with* a function $P : \Theta \rightarrow p(s)$, which assigns to each parameter point $\theta \in \Theta$ a probability distribution P_θ on *s*' (McCullough, p. 1225). Hence a statistical model is most abstractly defined as a function that ascribes to a specific element in some antecedent parametrization of the phenomenon a probability function from a family defined over the sample space. In other words, not only does a statistical model involve a whole family or set of probability functions, the model itself is best thought of as a composite or multiple function from parameters into probabilities. In many statistical models this composite complex entity already presupposes the sorts of distinctions characteristic of the tripartite conception, since it involves parametrizations (representing propensities) and probability distributions (single-case chances) and is intended to account for, or embed, models of experimental data (frequencies).

In applying or building a *probability model*, the most sensitive judgement concerns the selection of the sample space. And indeed, it is a well-known philosophical lesson that choosing the appropriate sample space – that is, selecting the outcome events or types that are to go into the space – is critical, and that the choice may importantly alter the properties of the model description. Statisticians, by contrast, see this selection as the final and simpler stage in a more complex modelling process, one that requires first of all to judiciously choose an appropriate parametrization of the phenomenon, secondly to choose the probability distributions that best correspond to each parameter, and only thirdly, and consequently, to choose the sample spaces. The 'art of statistical modelling' concerns all of these stages, and it is mainly the most sensitive first two stages that David Cox has in mind when he writes (Cox, 2006, p. 197): 'Formalization [...] is clearly of critical importance. It translates a subject-matter question into a formal statistical question and that translation must be reasonably faithful and, as far as is feasible, the consistency of the model with the data must be checked. How this translation from subject-matter problem to statistical model is done is often the most critical part of the analysis.'

In many cases of statistical modelling in the natural, life, and social sciences, the first parametrization stage is where considerations regarding dispositional properties in the chance set-ups – or propensities – enter. Thus, the relationship between the parameter and the sample spaces (Θ, s) is at the heart of the distinct roles of propensities and chances in the CNC. It makes sense to discuss those roles in the light of the second distinguishing feature of statistical models, namely their dynamical character, to which we now turn.

12 Two Types of Statistical Modelling

In a typical statistical model in the natural sciences, the relevant parameters include time, and the parametrized description will be time dependent. As a result, the probability functions will be dynamical and evolve in time in accordance with some law, often described in a differential or master equation. Statistical models differ on account of the kind of laws that they employ, and I shall in particular distinguish two kinds, reserving the term *pure probabilistic model* for those that are endowed with a deterministic dynamics only, while employing *pure stochastic model* for those that obey exclusively an indeterministic dynamics. Many models are hybrid and include deterministic and indeterministic laws. Hence statistical models lie on a spectrum from pure probabilism to pure stochasticity. By investigating both pure types we also investigate the end extremes of this spectrum.

12.1 Pure Probabilism: The Method of Arbitrary Functions

The main aim of many statistical models is to generate chance distributions over the outcome space that to a good approximation match the frequencies observed in experiments run on the modelled systems. This amounts to a type of explanation of the resulting frequencies that suits Nina Emery's explanatory requirement on chances (Emery, 2015, 2017). If the dynamics in the model is deterministic, the laws on their own cannot provide those chances – a deterministic law may only generate probabilities out of probabilities. Hence a *probabilistic* model (a statistical model with a deterministic dynamics) can only dynamically explain statistical phenomena if it acts on a set of probability distributions over the initial conditions of the system. Many systems generating statistical phenomena at the macro level (including most well-known games of chance, such as dice, roulette, etc.) are on the face of it deterministic, since they obey classical mechanical or Newtonian laws. How can probabilistic models account for such phenomena?

A long and distinguished tradition in mathematical physics provides a template. The method of arbitrary functions (MAF) begins with von Kries and Poincaré at the turn of the nineteenth century, and it remains relevant today in important work in mathematical statistics.[22] The central idea in the MAF is the thought that some systems are dynamically stable or invariant under permutations (within some range given by some formal constraints) of the initial probability distributions over the initial conditions of the system. In other words, the probability distributions over the outcome events are independent of the distribution over the initial conditions; they rather mainly depend only on the precise form of the deterministic dynamics. The phenomena modelled by MAF are thus in some sense the converse of chaotic phenomena: while the latter exhibit extreme sensitivity to (small variations in) initial conditions, the former display extreme resilience from (changes in the probability distributions over the) initial conditions.

The MAF is a method that falls well within the kind of more complex parametrized dynamical modelling practice that I have here referred to as 'statistical' modelling. Another, more specific reason to discuss it is that it furnishes a genuine dynamic probabilistic model for the paradigmatic example that I have been employing for a chance system, the coin toss. Keller (1986) provides the most sophisticated treatment, which employs a highly idealized parametrized description of the phenomenon – what this Element urges as the essential first stage in any statistical model. There are a number of idealizing assumptions involved because the model purports to reduce the set of free parameters to just two: the initial upwards velocity at which the coin is spun at its ejection (v), and the angular momentum through its trajectory (ω). To achieve such a reduction of the relevant dynamical variables a streamlined parametrized description is needed of what is in reality a more complex phenomenon. These idealizations allow the modeller to neglect every dynamical variable other than those representing the relevant propensities (see Figure 1), and include:

– The coin's radius is a and it remains constant throughout its motion.
– The coin is assumed to be of negligible thickness, or infinitely flat.
– Hence the coin's geometrical centre is its centre of gravity.
– At every instant t through its motion, the coin's centre of gravity finds itself at $y(t) = x$.
– At the initial stage $t = 0$ the coin finds itself at precisely height a: $y(0) = a$.

---

[22] See Von Plato (1985) for a historical review and Engel (1992) for state-of-the-art methodology.

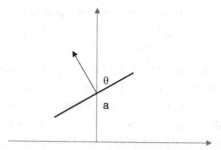

Figure 1 (adapted from Keller, 1986): The y-axis marks height, the x-axis marks time. The coin radius is a; the coin diameter is $2a$. The centre of the coin stands at a distance a from the floor. The angle subtended by the head side to the y-axis is θ.

- At the end of the motion, the coin's landing position is final (no rebound).
- Air friction is negligible; and the coin is not slowed down as a result.
- The coin's angular velocity is constant throughout its motion: $\frac{d^2\theta(t)}{dt^2} = 0$, where θ is the angle subtended to the upwards motion.

It is then possible to show, by applying classical mechanical equations of motion, that any arbitrary distribution over the initial upwards velocity v and angular velocity ω, as long as it fulfils minimal requirements, yields a final probability distribution over the Heads and Tails outcomes, which in the case of a fair coin (i.e. one not bent) is the equiprobable: Prob (H) = Prob (T) = ½. The requirements receive different names in the literature, and they have been the object of a considerable and intricate discussion.[23] The relevant point here is that a parametrization is implicit already in the selection of the relevant quantities that the initial probability functions will range over.

In other words, the ascription of probabilities to the possible Heads (H) and Tails (T) outcomes of a given coin-tossing experiment is not the result of a simple application of the principle of indifference, or any other variety of a principle of sufficient reason. Philosophers sometimes assume that the principle of indifference on its own will yield probability ½ for each possible outcome of the toss of a fair coin. A 'probability' model is just such an ascription of probabilities (i.e. prob (H) = prob (T) = 0,5) on the basis of indifference. There is not any need for any dynamical model of coin tossing

---

[23] Poincaré (1912) and Hopf (1932) explicitly require that the initial distribution functions be 'continuous' and the dynamics be such as to wash out the differences between any such functions. Strevens (2003) and Abrams (2012) propose versions of these requirements, called the 'macro-linearity' and 'micro-constancy' conditions. All these approaches have identical consequences for our purposes.

in order to arrive at the conclusion: a simple inspection of the geometrical properties of the coin would do. By contrast, a 'statistical' model of the phenomenon of coin tossing will necessarily be much more involved. A coin may well be perfectly symmetrical and fair in the sense that its outcomes are equiprobable; but the reason for the fairness of the coin is not, in a statistical model, to be found in the symmetries of the object. It is rather to be found, as in Keller's model, in the complex dynamics of the entire coin-tossing phenomenon under a suitable idealized parametrization. The system as modelled is not a thing, or entity, at a given time, but a rather complex dynamical process evolving in time, as described under a set of relevant parameters – endowed with certain propensities.

To sum up, the MAF employs what I have called *pure probabilistic* models. These are models of systems that yield a stable or resilient probability distribution over macroscopic variables of their chance set-up solely out of some deterministic dynamics acting on a range of distribution functions over initial microscopic variables of the system:

$$p_i \begin{cases} s_1 \\ s_2 \\ s_3 \end{cases} \rightarrow Law_{deterministic} \rightarrow p_f \begin{cases} o_1 \\ o_2 \end{cases}$$

The critical feature of MAF models is their ability to generate resiliently the same probability function, given the same parametrization of the phenomenon, as ideally described. A different probability function p'_i would result only out of a different parametrization, with a distinct set of initial conditions $\{s'_1, s'_2, \ldots, s'_n\}$, in turn resulting from a different set of idealizations in the model:

$$p'_i \begin{cases} s'_1 \\ s'_2 \\ s'_3 \end{cases} \rightarrow Law_{deterministic} \rightarrow p'_f \begin{cases} o_1 \\ o_2 \end{cases}$$

For instance, in the case of coin tossing, this entails relaxing the idealization that the coin is fair, for example, because the coin is no longer modelled as infinitely flat, or as having its centre of gravity at the geometrical centre, or because it is assumed to be experiencing precession, and hence its angular velocity is far from constant.[24] Most games of chance may be modelled in this fashion – and the methodology extends further to complex systems with underlying deterministic dynamics (Strevens, 2003, 2013). The invariance of the output probabilities under changes in initial conditions, given

---

[24] See Diaconis et al. (2007) for some of the relevant de-idealizations.

a parametrization, is indicative of stable single-case chances, those precisely grounded upon the propensities of the system and set-up; while the breakdown in invariance elicited by a new parametrization introduced in response to changes in the system's physical properties suggests that a change in the underlying propensities brings about corresponding changes in the chances.[25] This expresses the sort of counterfactually robust dependence typical of the explanatory relation sought after.

12.2 Pure Stochasticity: Indeterministic Dynamical Modelling

By contrast, in a *pure stochastic* statistical model the probabilities emerge out of the dynamics by itself, without recourse to any initial probability distributions over initial micro- or macroscopic conditions:

$$\begin{cases} s_1 \\ s_2 \\ s_3 \end{cases} \rightarrow Law_{stochastic} \rightarrow p_f \begin{cases} o_1 \\ o_2 \end{cases}$$

The laws in pure stochastic models are indeterministic or stochastic and generate objective probability distributions over the outcome events out of very precise specifications of the actual initial state of the system. The probability functions P_f predicted by such models are hardly ever invariant under changes in initial conditions – they are therefore sensitive not just to the parametrization entailed by the idealized description of a system, but also to the initial probability functions themselves, including their sample spaces. Since the underlying dynamics is not deterministic, these cases tend to lie outside the domain of ordinary macroscopic phenomena. Two examples include collapse interpretations in quantum mechanics and stochastic models for genetic variance in evolutionary theory.

Collapse theories in quantum mechanics assume an indeterministic change of the state of a quantum system (its wavefunction) either as a result of interaction with the open environment (as in quantum state diffusion or QSD theory) or spontaneously with a certain frequency (as in the so-called Ghirardi–Rimini–Weber or GRW theory). The overall dynamics is not deterministic; the changes

---

[25] There is nonetheless some debate regarding the nature of the distribution function over the initial conditions in MAF. Strevens (2013) and Abrams (2012, 2015) regard it as some kind of objective frequency, while Myrvold (2012) interprets it as a subjective probability reflecting an agent's degrees of belief over the exact initial conditions. This would reduce the propensity base of the chance ascription to only the features in the coin and the toss that are relevant to the distribution given the uncertainty over the initial conditions; it would also provide yet another, third, sense in which 'subjective' considerations are necessary to determine objective probabilities (I thank an anonymous referee for the observation).

in the values of the dynamical quantities are rather sudden and stochastic: one can only determine their probability in the form of either transition probabilities or relaxation times. Thus, for example, a model for a quantum state diffusion process is a statistical model that yields continuous probability distributions for the evolution of the state in an abstract space, such as a Bloch space. As such the motion of the state vector in the space appears random when as a matter of fact it is highly constrained by the probabilistic equations of motion. Gisin and Percival (1992, p. 5679) make it clear that these equations derive from a master equation including a drift term and stochastic fluctuations, and they are therefore irreducibly indeterministic: '[...] there can be no general deterministic equation for the pure states ψ. But there are stochastic equations, as might be expected from the probabilistic nature of the interaction with the environment. In time dt the variation $d\psi$ in ψ is then given by the Itô form: $d\psi = vdt + \sum_j u_j d\xi_j$, where vdt is the drift term and the differential stochastic fluctuations are represented by a sum over independent Wiener processes'. The process may be understood as a sort of random walk on the Bloch sphere where states are represented: the QSD models are 'purely stochastic' in our terminology.

The Ghirardi–Rimini–Weber (GRW) theory is similar except that it does not require open systems in constant interaction with the environment but rather postulates stochastic and spontaneous 'shocks' on the wavefunction which bring it regularly into the eigenstates of macroscopically well-defined observables. The relaxation times are construed in such a way that any finite-time observation on any macroscopic composite typically yields a definite outcome. There is no macroscopic superposition due to the aggregate of the non-linear stochastic terms added to the Schrödinger dynamics. The GRW modification of the dynamics in effect 'leaves things unchanged for microscopic objects, while, for macroscopic objects, it transforms quantum mechanics into a stochastic mechanics in phase space exhibiting the classical features' (Ghirardi et al., 1986, p. 34). This somehow inverts the traditional picture, since the Schrödinger equation is a deterministic equation on the wavefunction; while the GRW theory presupposes that the fundamental stochastic collapses it postulates for the wavefunction manifest themselves at the macro level. Since GRW fixes the nature of the 'shocks' in terms of a universal constant, it is plausible to think of it as providing a mixed statistical model, which is not purely probabilistic nor purely stochastic, but a mixture of both.[26]

---

[26] For a discussion of the propensities involved in GRW, see Frigg and Hoefer (2007) or Suárez (2007, pp. 432–3)

Another field that illustrates statistical modelling in its stochastic variety is evolutionary biology – particularly population genetics, but more generally in the study of variability across populations, or in ecosystems. As for the former, consider the celebrated Wright–Fisher model for genetic drift.[27] The model describes the time-evolution of a population of N genes, under considerably strong idealizing conditions. For instance, it assumes that populations are finite and do not vary in size from one to the next generation, and that the generations do not overlap – they are replaced wholesale every time. According to this model, the number of alleles in generation $g + 1$ is obtained by drawing with replacement from the gene population in the previous generation g. Thus if there are i alleles of type A in generation g, then the number of type A alleles in generation $g + 1$ has a binomial distribution yielding a Markov process or chain with a transition matrix given as $P_{ij} = \binom{N}{j}\left(\frac{i}{N}\right)^j\left(1 - \frac{i}{N}\right)^{N-j}$, for $0 \leq i, j \leq N$. Each expression for i, j provides a transition probability for the number of alleles in a later generation.

The model can be refined and extended by suitably weakening the idealizations and varying the range of parameters. Kimura (1968) introduced the hypothesis of neutrality: some gene mutations have no effect whatever on fitness, and hence such alleles cannot vary out of natural selection; so genetic drift must account for a larger share of gene pool variability than previously thought. This invites the thought that the idealizations in the original Wright–Fisher model may be too strong. A new stochastic model then developed allowing for overlaps amongst generational populations. Once again, a parametrization of the phenomenon, under some idealized description, is critical in order to establish the appropriate probability functions and their domains. Many models in evolutionary biology are neither purely probabilistic, nor purely stochastic, but lie somewhere in the spectrum.[28]

13 Towards a Methodology of Chance Explanation

Statistical modelling is a complex activity that centres around providing explanatory as well as descriptive models for observed or presumed correlation phenomena. The models invoke dynamical laws and employ particular

---

[27] For an exposition see Blythe and McKane (2007) or the seminal Fisher (1930).

[28] Rice (2008). It must be noted that most phenomena underdetermine the type of model that they can be represented by – and in particular whether a 'pure probability' or a 'pure stochastic' model – see Werndl (2013). Hence, not surprisingly, some philosophers have claimed genetic drift is best modelled by means of what I would call a 'pure probability' model. See Strevens (2003, 2016) for some excellent discussion of the issues involved, including a similar distinction between parameters and variables as applied to micro-constancy.

parametrizations, often describing the phenomena in a highly idealized form. Whether the laws employed are deterministic or stochastic, the models appear to have an explanatory role. This often reflects the fact that the idealized parametrizations represent the underlying mechanisms, causal powers, or capacities operating in the system as the models' essential posits in the 'nexus of chance'.

The explanans employs an idealized description of the propensities – or probabilistic dispositions – inherent in the system. As the idealizations change, so do the required parametrizations, and the ensuing description of the chances generated in the system. A biased or precessing coin has distinct chances to land heads or tails if tossed, and it must be modelled so; the propensities of an open quantum system in interaction with the environment are displayed in a chance distribution to localize as a result; gene populations possess certain propensities to pass on types of alleles to the next generation with a given chance; and so on. In all these cases, there is a complex relation between (i) the propensities in the systems or chance set-ups, as revealed in the parametrization employed; (ii) the chances yielded over the outcome events, often at a macroscopic level; and (iii) the frequencies that are presumed or observed in experimental runs, which provide the empirical basis for our chance claims, and which are ultimately the object of our models' explanation.

This is the nexus of chance in action; its distinct parts (propensities, chances, frequencies) are all required in order to make sense of the methodology employed in statistical modelling. The order of explanation seems to entail a distinct hierarchy, with the propensities at the highest level of explanation, the chances as the dynamical consequences of the propensities, and the finite frequencies as the putative consequences or explananda. Most minimally, the explanation is a variety of the model explanations that have been recently discussed in the literature (Bokulich, 2008). The essential explanatory posits in these models are precisely the components in the nexus of chance: propensities, understood as probabilistic dispositions, give rise within the highly idealized model descriptions to chance distributions over the outcomes; these in turn imply certain finite frequencies in particular experimental set-ups, which are counterfactually robust in pre-established ways. This is to say that they provide explanations for the finite frequencies observed, or their generalizations in data models. To the extent that a phenomenon P is minimally explained by the essential posits of a successful model representation for it, it follows that the nexus of chance is involved essentially in all of these explanations.

The *complex nexus of chance* (CNC) only confronts the question of the nature of chance indirectly – and, as we saw in Section 10, a number of options remain open. It assumes that objective probability is a complex and plural notion, requiring us to consider the interaction in modelling practice of its distinct parts – propensities, chances, frequencies – while refusing to reduce any of them, or indeed the whole complex nexus, to just one of its parts. Does this plural and pragmatist attitude to objective probability enable a different inquiry into the nature of chance?

Whilst there is no doubt that some new avenues open up for such types of inquiries, the safe and more limited conclusion of this section is this: regardless of what the ontology of chance in fact is, the methodology of chance explanations via statistical models presupposes a plural metaphysics of chance and a pragmatist outlook on its application. The CNC thus becomes a constraint on any further inquiry. There are arguments in favour of this conclusion coming from the irreducibility of chances to either propensity or frequency. But the most significant argument for pragmatic pluralism about objective probability derives from scientific modelling practice itself. CNC is the interlinked set of practices that employ dispositional probabilities – or propensities – as the grounds for the formal probability distributions over outcome spaces typical of chancy phenomena. This suggests that no serious philosophical inquiry into the nature of chance can start from very different assumptions. For instance, any philosophical inquiry that presupposes a unique ontology would need to painstakingly explain away why the methodology of statistical modelling is on the face of it so strikingly diverse in its assumptions.

There is by now an entrenched view in the philosophy of science that scientific knowledge does not just reduce to abstract hypothetical theory and concrete observable data, but that a lot of our knowledge is contained in between – in approximations, idealizations, models of the data and phenomena, and all sorts of modelling techniques involved. The distinction between theories, phenomena, and data originates in Suppes (1962) and is further developed by Bogen and Woodward (1988), while the claim that there are autonomous models that mediate between theory and the world goes back to Morgan and Morrison (1999). There is a sense, which I have explored elsewhere (Suárez, 2017a), in which the tripartite conception of objective probability that I advance in this Element as part of a defence of the CNC reflects the above distinctions in general philosophy of science and modelling. Theories are not tested directly in comparisons with bare data, but via mediating models of the phenomena, which are in turn not mere descriptions, but autonomous and creative generalizations of the data. Similarly, in the CNC propensities (understood as dispositional properties of chance setups) are not tested against finite frequency data, but against probability distributions within statistical models of the phenomena. These models are similarly autonomous and creative, requiring a very developed sense of practical fit and involving complex and highly educated judgements regarding the choices of descriptions (parametrizations) of the general phenomena of interest.

The formal concept of probability plays a critical role in representing the single-case chances that mediate between theoretical descriptions of mechanisms, machines, or complex dispositional set-ups, on the one hand, and frequency data obtained under constrained experimental conditions, on the other. This formal concept has been tailored to its role as a universal tool in statistical modelling, but what it represents in reality remains elusive. A number of philosophical approaches are available, and the suggestion in this Element is that there may be no univocal essence to chance functions, or formal probabilities, other than their ubiquitous practical role in the application of statistical models. And just as mediating models (Morgan and Morrison, 1999) cannot be reduced to either pure theoretical knowledge or bare experimental data, similarly chance and objective probability cannot be reduced to either propensity or frequency. From this point of view, the failure of reductive projects about chance and objective probability is hardly surprising.

Together propensities and chances can be employed to account for, or to explain (in a minimal sense of model explanation), the kind of finite frequency data so common in experimental runs on chance set-ups. In this respect, statistical modelling is no different from any other form of scientific modelling practice. A large part of what is required in understanding chance is related to understanding the practice of statistical modelling. There are positive and negative reasons that support this conclusion, and they all have been canvassed in this Element. The first half of the Element made a case for a dual concept of probability through history, one that does not grant a univocal understanding of probability. There are both objective and subjective probabilities in the world, and moreover they both play a role in any philosophical understanding of either. The second half of the Element argued that the very practice of statistical modelling supports a plural metaphysics for objective probability – the tripartite conception – together with a pragmatist approach to the methodologies involved in its application in practice.

The overall take-up of this Element is then that understanding chance requires us not just to engage in philosophical interpretation. The first half of the Element led the reader through the morass of the historical development of probability and its implications for an interpretational stance on chance. While this is valuable work, which ultimately shows that propensities, chances, and frequencies ought to be kept distinct, an understanding of objective probability from a functional pragmatic perspective is also required. If we want to understand chance fully, we need to study its *uses* both in historical terms and in terms of how it is applied nowadays in the sciences. The second half of the Element continued the argument for pluralism, this time as applied to objective probability only. It argued that objective probability itself must be understood as involving a tripartite distinction between propensities, single-case chances, and frequencies. It then went on to add a pragmatist thesis regarding the uses of this tripartite conception in modelling practice (CNC). What CNC shows, I suggest, is the importance of what Deborah Mayo (2018, p. 13) calls 'statistical philosophy': the study of the complex nexus of principles, methods, and interpretations involved in actual statistical practice. This study has the promise to shed light upon foundational issues regarding the nature of objective probability, and it should complement the more traditional epistemological and ontological approaches to the nature of chance.

References

Abrams, M. (2012). Mechanistic probability. *Synthese* **187** (2), 343–75.

Abrams, M. (2015). Equidynamics and reliable inference about frequencies. *Metascience* **24**, 173–88.

Berkovitz, J. (2015). The propensity interpretation of probability: A re-evaluation. *Erkenntnis* **80**, 1–83.

Bertrand, J. (1889). *Calcul de Probabilités*, Paris: Gauthier Villards.

Bird, A. (Forthcoming). A simple introduction to epidemiological modelling – The SIR model. Available at: https://philosophyandmedicine.org/events/lay persons-guide-to-epidemiological-modelling/.

Blythe, R., and A. J. McKane (2007). Stochastic models of evolution in genetics, ecology and linguistics. *Journal of Statistical Mechanics: Theory and Experiment* **7**, P07018.

Bogen, J., and J. Woodward (1988). Saving the phenomena. *The Philosophical Review* **97** (3), 303–52.

Bokulich, A. (2008). Explanatory fictions. In M. Suárez, ed., *Fictions in Science: Philosophical Essays on Modelling and Idealization*, Routledge, pp. 91–109.

Borel, E. (1909). *Elements de la Théorie des Probabilités*, Paris: A. Heinmann & Fils.

Carnap, R. (1945). The two concepts of probability: The problem of probability. *Philosophy and Phenomenological Research* **5** (4), 513–32.

Carnap, R. (1950). *Logical Foundations of Probability*, Chicago: University of Chicago Press.

Cartwright, N. (1989). *Nature's Capacities and Their Measurement*, Oxford: Oxford University Press.

Cartwright, N. (1999). *The Dappled World: A Study of the Boundaries of Science*, Cambridge: Cambridge University Press.

Cox, D. R. (2006). *Principles of Statistical Inference*, Cambridge: Cambridge University Press.

Daston, L. (1988). *Classical Probability in the Enlightenment*, Princeton: Princeton University Press.

De Finetti, B. (1937). 'La prévision: ses lois logiques, ses sources subjectives.' *Annales de l'Institut Henri Poincaré*, 7, 1–68

De Finetti, B. (2008). *Philosophical Lectures on Probability*, Alberto Mura, ed., Dordrecht: Springer. (English version of De Finetti, B. (1995), *Filosofia della Probabilitá*, Milan: Il Saggiatore).

Diaconis, P., et al. (2007). Dynamical bias in the coin toss. *Society for Industrial and Applied Mathematics* (SIAM review) **49** (2), 211–35.

Eagle, A. (2004). Twenty-one arguments against propensity interpretations of probability. *Erkenntnis* **60** (3), 371–416.

Emery, N. (2015). Chance, possibility, and explanation. *British Journal for the Philosophy of Science* **66** (1), 95–120.

Emery, N. (2017). A naturalist guide to objective chance. *Philosophy of Science* **84** (3), 480–99.

Engel, E. (1992). *A Road to Randomness in Physical Systems*, Berlin: Springer-Verlag.

Fetzer, J. (1993). Peirce and propensities. In Moore, ed., *Charles S. Peirce and the Philosophy of Science*. Tuscaloosa:Alabama University Press, pp. 60–71.

Fisher, R. A. (1930). *The Genetical Theory of Natural Selection*, Oxford: Clarendon Press.

Frigg, R., and C. Hoefer (2007). Probability in GRW theory. *Studies in the History and Philosophy of Modern Physics* **38** (2), 371–89.

Gelman, A., and C. Hennig (2017). Beyond subjective and objective in statistics. *J. R. Statist. Soc. A* **180** (4), 967–1033.

Ghirardi, G. C., A. Rimini, and T. Weber (1986). Unified dynamics for microscopic and macroscopic systems. *Physical Review D* **34** (2), 470–91.

Gigerenzer, G., et al. (1989). *The Empire of Chance: How Probability Changed Science and Everyday Life*, Cambridge: Cambridge University Press.

Gillies, D. (2000). *Philosophical Theories of Probability*, London: Routledge.

Gisin, N., and I. C. Percival (1992). The quantum state diffusion model applied to open systems. *Journal of Physics A: Math Gen* **25**, 5677.

Goodman, N. (1955). *Fact, Fiction and Forecast*, Cambridge: Harvard University Press.

Hacking, I. (1975). *The Emergence of Probability*, Cambridge: Cambridge University Press.

Hacking, I. (1990). *The Taming of Chance*, Cambridge: Cambridge University Press.

Hájek, A. (1997). 'Mises redux' – redux: Fifteen arguments against finite frequentism. *Erkenntnis* **45** (2/3), 209–27.

Hájek, A. (2003). What conditional probability could not be. *Synthese* **137**, 273–323.

Hájek, A. (2009). Fifteen arguments against hypothetical frequentism. *Erkenntnis* **70**, 211–35.

Heesterbeek, J. A. P. (2002). A brief history of R_O and a recipe for its calculation. *Acta Biotheoretica* **50**, 189–204.

Hewitt, E., and L. J. Savage (1955). Symmetric measures on Cartesian products. *Trans. Amer. Math. Soc.* **80**, 470–501.

Hoefer, C. (2018). *Chance in the World: A Humean Guide to Objective Chance*, Oxford: Oxford University Press.

Hopf, E. (1932). On causality, statistics and probability. *Journal of Mathematics and Physics*, **13**, 51–102.

Howson, C., and Urbach, P. (2006). *Scientific Reasoning: The Bayesian Approach*, Open Court Publishing (3rd edition).

Humphreys, P. (1985). Why propensities cannot be probabilities. *The Philosophical Review* **94** (4), 557–70.

Humphreys, P. (1989). *The Chances of Explanation*, Princeton: Princeton University Press.

Ismael, J. (2008). Raid! The big, bad bug dissolved. *Nous* **42** (2), 292–307.

Ismael, J. (Forthcoming). On chance (or why I am only a half-Humean). In Kleinberg, S., ed., *Time and Causation in the Sciences*, Cambridge: Cambridge University Press.

Keller, J. (1986). The probability of heads. *American Math. Monthly*, **93**, 191–7.

Kermack, W. O., and A. G. McKendrick (1927). A contribution to the mathematical theory of epidemics. *Proceedings of the Royal Society of Medicine*, **115A**, 700–21.

Keynes, J. M. (1921). *A Treatise on Probability*, Cambridge: Cambridge University Press.

Kimura, M. (1968). *The Neutral Theory of Molecular Evolution*, Cambridge: Cambridge University Press.

Kolmogorov, A. N. (1933). *Foundations of the Theory of Probability*, London: Chelsea Books (2nd edition, 1956).

Kucharski, A. (2020). *The Rules of Contagion: Why Things Spread and Why They Stop*, London: Profile Books.

Laplace, P. S. (1814). *A Philosophical Essay on Probabilities*, trans. F. W. Truscott and F. L. Emory, New York: Dover.

Lewis, D. (1980). A subjectivist guide to objective chance. In D. Lewis (1986), *Philosophical Papers*, vol. 2, Oxford: Oxford University Press, pp. 83–113.

Loewer, B. (2004). David Lewis' Humean theory of objective chance. *Philosophy of Science*, **71**, 1115–25.

Lyon, A. (2011). Deterministic probability: Neither chance nor credence. *Synthese* **182**: 413–32.

Mayo, D. (1996). *Error and the Growth of Experimental Knowledge*, Chicago: University of Chicago Press.

Mayo, D. (2018). *Statistical Inference as Severe Testing: How to Get beyond the Statistics Wars*, Cambridge: Cambridge University Press.

McCullough, P. (2002). What is a statistical model? *Annals of Statistics* **30** (5), 1225–310.

Mellor, H. (2005). *Probability: A Philosophical Introduction*, London: Routledge.

Moran, P. (1959). Random processes in genetics. *Proc. Cambridge Philos. Society*, **54**, 60–72.

Morgan, M., and M. Morrison (1999). *Mediating Models: Perspectives on Natural and Social Sciences*, Cambridge: Cambridge University Press.

Myrvold, W. C. (2012). Deterministic laws and epistemic chances. In Ben-Menahem and M. Hemmo (eds.), *Probability in Physics*, The Frontiers Collection. Berlin: Springer Verlag, pp. 73–85.

Peirce, C. S. (1893). Reply to the necessitarians. *The Monist* **3**, 526–70.

Peirce, C. S. (1910). Note on the doctrine of chances. In *Philosophical Writings of Peirce*, New York: Dover.

Poincaré, H. (1912). *Calcul de Probabilités*, 2nd ed., Paris: Gauthier Villars (1st ed., 1898).

Popper, K. (1957), "The Propensity Interpretation of the Calculus of Probability and the Quantum Theory," in Stephan Körner, ed., *Observation and Interpretation in the Philosophy of Physics*, New York: Dover, pp. 65–70.

Ramsey, F. P. (1926). Truth and probability. In *The Foundations of Mathematics and Other Logical Essays*, Cambridge: Cambridge University Press.

Reichenbach, H. (1915/2008). *The Concept of Probability*, Open Court Publishers.

Reichenbach, H. (1935/49). *The Theory of Probability: An Inquiry into the Logical and Mathematical Foundations of the Calculus of Probability*, Berkeley: University of California Press.

Renyi, A. (1955). On a new axiomatic theory of probability. *Acta Mathematica Academiae Scientiae Hungaricae*, vol. 6, 286–335.

Rice, S. H. (2008). A stochastic version of the Price equation reveals the interplay of deterministic and stochastic processes in evolution. *BMC Evolutionary Biology*, **8**, 262.

Ross, R. (1910). *The Prevention of Malaria*, London: Murray.

Rowbottom, D. (2013), 'Bertrand's paradox revisited: Why Bertrand's "solutions" are all inapplicable', *Philosophia Mathematica* (III), **21**, 110–14.

Salmon, W. (1979). Propensities: A discussion review. *Erkenntnis*, **14**, 183–216.

Savage, L. J. (1954). *The Foundations of Statistics*, New York: Dover.

Skyrms, B. (1977). Resiliency, propensities, and causal necessity. *The Journal of Philosophy*, **LXXIV** (11), 704–13.

Sober, E. (2010). Evolutionary theory and the reality of macro-probabilities. In
E. Eels and J. Fetzer, eds., *The Place or Probability in Science*. Dordrecht:
Springer, pp. 133–60.

Stoppard, T. (1969). *Rosencrantz and Guildenstern Are Dead*. London: Faber
and Faber.

Strevens, M. (2003). *Bigger than Chaos: Understanding Complexity through
Probability*, Cambridge, MA: Harvard University Press.

Strevens, M. (2013). *Tychomancy: Inferring Probability from Causal Structure*.
Cambridge, MA: Harvard University Press.

Strevens, M. (2016). The reference class problem in evolutionary biology:
Distinguishing selection from drift. In G. Ramsey and C. Pence, eds.,
Chance in Evolution, Chicago: University of Chicago Press, pp. 145–75.

Suárez, M. (2007). Quantum propensities. *Studies in the History and
Philosophy of Modern Physics* **38** (2), 418–38.

Suárez, M. (2013). Propensities and pragmatism. *The Journal of Philosophy*,
CX (2), 61–92.

Suárez, M. (2017a). Propensities, probabilities, and experimental statistics. In
M. Massimi, J. W. Romeijn, and G. Schurz (eds.), *EPSA15: Selected Papers:
European Studies in Philosophy of Science*, **5**, pp. 335–45.

Suárez, M. (2017b). Comment on Gelman and Hennig, *Journal of the Royal
Statistical Society A*, **180** (4), 1020–1.

Suárez, M. (2018). The chances of propensities. *British Journal for the
Philosophy of Science*, **69**, 1155–77.

Suppes, P. (1962). Models of data. In E. Nagel, P. Suppes, and A. Tarski (eds.),
*Logic, Methodology and Philosophy of Science: Proceedings of the 1960
International Congress*. Reprinted in Suppes, P. (1969), *Studies in the
Methodology and Foundations of Science: Selected Papers from 1951 to
1969*, Dordrecht: Springer, pp. 24–35.

Van Fraassen, B. (1993). *Quantum Mechanics: An Empiricist View*, Oxford:
Oxford University Press.

Venn, J. (1866). *The Logic of Chance*, London: McMillan.

von Mises, R. (1928/1957). *Probability, Statistics and Truth*, 2nd ed. (1957),
London: Allen & Unwin.

von Plato, J. (1985). The method of arbitrary functions. *British Journal for the
Philosophy of Science*, **34** (1), 37–47.

Werndl, C. (2013). On choosing between deterministic and indeterministic
models: Underdetermination and indirect evidence. *Synthese*, **190** (12),
2243–65.

Williamson, J. (2010). *In Defence of Objective Bayesianism*. Oxford: Oxford
University Press.

Acknowledgements

For comments I want to thank Hernán Bobadilla, Carl Hoefer, Michael Strevens, and audiences at Paris (IHPST Panthéon-Sorbonne, 2017 and 2018), Turin (conference on the models of explanation in 2018), and Pittsburgh (HPS annual lecture series 2018–19), as well as two referees for Cambridge University Press. My thanks also to Jacob Stegenga, Robert Northcott, and Annie Toynbee at Cambridge University Press for their editorial encouragement and advice. Financial support is acknowledged from the European Commission (Marie Curie grant project 329430 (FP7-PEOPLE-2012-IEF)) and the Spanish government projects FFI2014-57064-P and PGC2018-099423-B-100.

Cambridge Elements ☰

Philosophy of Science

Robert Northcott
Birkbeck, University of London

Robert Northcott is Reader in Philosophy. He began at Birkbeck in the summer of 2011, and in 2017 became Head of Department. Before that, he taught for six years at the University of Missouri-St Louis. He received his PhD from the London School of Economics. Before switching to philosophy, Robert did graduate work in economics, receiving an MSc, and undergraduate work in mathematics and history.

Jacob Stegenga
University of Cambridge

Jacob Stegenga is a Reader in the Department of History and Philosophy of Science at the University of Cambridge. He has published widely on fundamental topics in reasoning and rationality and philosophical problems in medicine and biology. Prior to joining Cambridge he taught in the United States and Canada, and he received his PhD from the University of California San Diego.

About the Series

This series of Elements in Philosophy of Science provides an extensive overview of the themes, topics and debates which constitute the philosophy of science. Distinguished specialists provide an up-to-date summary of the results of current research on their topics, as well as offering their own take on those topics and drawing original conclusions.

Cambridge Elements ☰

Philosophy of Science

Printed in the United States
By Bookmasters